APPLIED PRINCIPLES OF FINANCE WORKBOOK

Preliminary Edition

J. Randall Woolridge, Ph.D
Gary Gray, Ph.D
Penn State University

KENDALL/HUNT PUBLISHING COMPANY
4050 Westmark Drive   Dubuque, Iowa 52002

Chapter 1

Introduction to
Applied Principles of Finance

Introduction to
Applied Principles of Finance

This module provides a general overview of the role of corporate finance in organizations today. The objectives of the session include:

(1) A knowledge of the expanding role of finance in business and the economy;

(2) An understanding of the three areas of finance -
       corporate finance, capital markets and financial institutions,
       and investments and valuation;

(3) An introduction to ten important principles that underlie the theory of finance;

(4) A discussion of the three basic sets of decisions that corporate managers face –
       the investment decision, the financing decision, and the dividend decision; and

(5) A familiarity with the tools in your financial toolbox.

Corporate Finance

Corporate Finance

Businesses

Investments

Financial **Institutions & Markets**

Financial Markets

Investors

The Ten Principles of Finance

- Principle 1: Higher Returns Require Taking More Risk
- Principle 2: Efficient Capital Markets are Tough to Beat
- Principle 3: Rational Investors are Risk Averse
- Principle 4: Supply and Demand Drive Stock Prices in the Short-run
- Principle 5: Corporate Finance and Governance:
  Corporate Managers Should Make Decisions That Maximize Shareholder Value

---

The Ten Principles of Finance

- Principle 6: Transaction Costs, Taxes and Inflation are Your Enemies
- Principle 7: Time and the Value of Money are Closely Related
- Principle 8: Asset Allocation is a Very Important Decision
- Principle 9: Asset Diversification Reduces Risk
- Principle 10: An Asset Pricing Model Should be Used to Value Investments

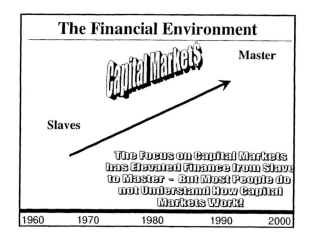

The Financial Environment

Capital Markets

Master

Slaves

The Focus on Capital Markets has Elevated Finance from Slave to Master – But Most People do not Understand How Capital Markets Work!

| 1960 | 1970 | 1980 | 1990 | 2000 |

Gamblers, Masters, and Slaves

The Primary Issues in Corporate Finance

1. What is a Firm Worth?

2. What Capital Structure Creates the Most Value?

3. Does the Cost of Capital for Firms Vary Between Countries, and if So, Why?

4. Does a Firm's Ownership Structure Affect the Answers to the First 3 Questions?

Financial Decisions and the Financial Tool Box

The Objective Function
Maximize the Value of the Firm

Basic Corporate Financial Decisions
1) The Investment Decision: Allocating scarce resources across competing uses?
2) The Financing Decision: Raising funds to finance these projects?
3) The Dividend Decision: Rreturning Funds to investors?

The Corporate Financial Toolbox

| Accounting Statements and Ratios | Present Value | Risk and Return Models | Spreadsheet Modelling |

Chapter 2

The Ten Principles of Finance

The Ten Principles of Finance

Chapter Overview

- Principle 1: Higher Returns Require Taking More Risk
- Principle 2: Efficient Capital Markets are Tough to Beat
- Principle 3: Rational Investors are Risk Averse
- Principle 4: Supply and Demand Drive Stock Prices in the Short-run
- Principle 5: Corporate Finance and Governance:
  Corporate Managers Should Make Decisions That Maximize Shareholder Value

---

The Ten Principles of Finance

Chapter Overview

- Principle 6: Transaction Costs, Taxes and Inflation are Your Enemies
- Principle 7: Time and the Value of Money are Closely Related
- Principle 8: Asset Allocation is a Very Important Decision
- Principle 9: Asset Diversification Reduces Risk
- Principle 10: An Asset Pricing Model Should be Used to Value Investments

The Ten Principles of Finance

<u>Principle 1</u>: Higher Returns Require Taking More Risk

- A trade-off exists between expected returns and risks on an investment
- Safe investments have low returns
- High returns require investors to take big risks
- Ibbotson and Sinquefield study of historical annual rates and distributions of returns on various classes of investments from Treasury bills to stocks shows the direct relationship between the expected return of an asset and the risk associated with receiving that return

The Ten Principles of Finance

Higher Returns Require Taking More Risk

The results of the Ibbotson and Sinquefield study is shown below:

	Return	Std Dev.
Treasury Bills	3.8%	3.2%
Government Bonds	5.3%	9.4%
Corporate Bonds	5.8%	8.6%
Large Company Stock	10.7%	20.2%
Small Company Stock	12.5%	33.2%

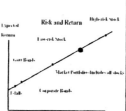

Probability of Reward versus Risk and Reversion to the Mean

S&P 500, DJIA, NASDAQ: 5-Year Stock Index Chart

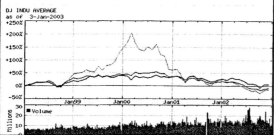

Probability of Reward versus Risk and Reversion to the Mean

Before you invest in an asset, you should assess whether the probabilities of reward or risk are equal or skewed.

Over time there is a tendency for returns and risk of asset markets to revert to average levels—reversion to the mean.

When stock prices are at relatively low levels by P/E ratios or P/BV ratios or P/S ratios, chances for a good return increase and the market is a *buy*.

When these ratios are at high levels, sell or avoid a buy.

Probability of Reward versus Risk and Reversion to the Mean

Over the long-run the returns associated with stocks have tracked their growth rate in earnings.

During the 1995-99 period the average return on the S&P 500 was 28.7%, and the average growth in earnings was under 10%.

During the late 90's prices of technology stocks were at levels that were much higher than their profits from operation could ever support.

Reversion to the mean suggests that the stock market run was unsustainable and much lower or negative returns were on the horizon to bring averages back into line with historic returns.

The Ten Principles of Finance

Principle 2: Efficient Capital Markets are Tough to Beat

- According to the theory of efficient capital markets (ECM): the stock market is brutally efficient; current stock prices reflect all publicly available information; and stock prices react completely, correctly, and almost instantaneously to incorporate the receipt of new information
- If the stock market is efficient, it would be useless to forecast future prices by technical analysis and fundamental analysis

What do we mean by Efficient Markets?

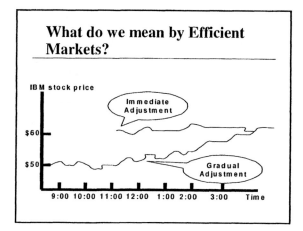

The Ten Principles of Finance

Efficient Capital Markets are Tough to Beat

- Various studies have been undertaken to test the notion of efficient capital markets and most of the studies have found results that were consistent with efficient capital markets

- However, Fama and French study found that stocks with a high book to market value ratio consistently outperformed stocks with low book to market ratios, p/e ratios and market capitalization considerations

- Even if some anomalies exist, capital markets are reasonably efficient and it is difficult for an investor to consistently beat the investment returns associated with a buy-and-hold strategy

Markets may not be all that efficient!

1992 Fama and French Stock Return Study
Portfolios Based on Ascending Book Equity/Market Equity Ratios

Portfolio	Monthly Return	Annualized Return	Avg. Number of Stocks	Weighted Avg. Return	Difference in Return
1A	0.30%	3.60%	89	14.99%	-11.39%
1B	0.67%	8.04%	98	14.99%	-6.95%
2	0.87%	10.44%	209	14.99%	-4.55%
3	0.97%	11.64%	222	14.99%	-3.35%
4	1.04%	12.48%	226	14.99%	-2.51%
5	1.17%	14.04%	230	14.99%	-0.95%
6	1.30%	15.60%	235	14.99%	0.61%
7	1.44%	17.28%	237	14.99%	2.29%
8	1.50%	18.00%	239	14.99%	3.01%
9	1.59%	19.08%	239	14.99%	4.09%
10A	1.92%	23.04%	120	14.99%	8.05%
10B	1.83%	21.96%	117	14.99%	6.97%
			2261		

F&F Study shows interesting anomaly

Fama & French Study

Annualized Return vs. Portfolios Sorted by Increasing (BE/ME) Ratio

Portfolio	Return
1	~3.5%
2	~8%
3	~10.5%
4	~12%
5	~12.5%
6	~14.5%
7	~16%
8	~17.5%
9	~18.5%
10	~19.5%
11	~23.5%
12	~22.5%

The Ten Principles of Finance

Principle 3: Rational Investors are Risk Averse

- Risk aversion means that a rational investor prefers less risk to more risk. "A bird in hand is worth two in the bush." "A safe dollar is worth more than a risky dollar."
- Finance theory is based upon the assumption that investors exhibit risk averse behavior
- A risk-averse investor does not avoid risk at all cost. He takes some small risks
- As an investor, it is important to determine your risk/return profile and identify favorable investments before investing

---

Normal Distributions of Returns

Normal Distribution with mean = 10.50% and standard deviation = 10.25%

Return: -20, -10, 0, 10, 20, 30, 40, 50

Return Distributions of Two Stocks

Normal Distribution with mean = 10.00% and standard deviation as indicated

Return

-15   -5   5   15   25   35

—— Std Dev = 10 —— Std Dev = 20

Rational Investors are Risk Averse

Risk aversion is a good trait.

Realize what type of investor you are and how much risk you can stomach and afford

Investor personality quizzes Appendix 2-A

Carefully research your choices and make investments that you believe are undervalued and have a higher probability of increasing in value than decreasing

The Ten Principles of Finance

Principle 4: Supply and Demand Drive Stock Prices in the Short-run

- The market price of a stock is determined by the interaction of the supply of stock by sellers and the demand for stock by buyers

- In the short-run, a stock's current price may be heavily influenced by a very temporary and extreme supply and demand imbalance or by the stock market's reaction to the receipt of new information and may not have anything to do with the true long-term value of a company

The Ten Principles of Finance

Supply and Demand Drive Stock Prices in the Short-run

- Current price is where the supply of stock intersects with the demand for stock
- Lower commissions of 90's greatly increased demand for stocks thereby driving up prices
- If investor demand for a type of company exists, investment bankers will partner with entrepreneurs to create the companies to fill the demand
- Eventually, supply will catch up to demand and when that occurs, demand inevitably falls

Supply and Demand Drive Stock Prices in the Short-run

JDSU 5-Year Stock Price Chart

JDS UNIPHASE as of 3-Jan-2003

Supply and Demand Drive Stock Prices in the Short-run

A stock's current price * outstanding shares equals market equity.

VA Linux up 733%, FreeMarkets, Akamai, CacheFlow up +400% at IPO.

ICGE example: $200.94 per share, 287.7 million shares = $57 billion assets worth less than 10% of that.

JDSU worth over $200 billion in 2000 and losing money?

Supply and Demand Drive Stock Prices in the Short-run

Current stock price reflects the amount that the marginal investor, given supply and demand considerations, is willing to pay to acquire as little as 100 shares of a company

In short-run this price may or may not have anything to do with the long-term value of the company.

Current price may be influenced by temporary supply and demand imbalance or by the markets over or under reaction to information.--ENMD

The Ten Principles of Finance

Principle 5: Corporate Finance and Governance: *Corporate Managers Should Make Decisions That Maximize Shareholder Value*

- Management Has Fiduciary Responsibility to Act In Shareholder's Interests
- Shareholder Value Approach Favors Strategies That Enhance Company's Cash-Flow Generating Ability
- Creating Shareholder Value Minimizes Value Gaps

Corporate Managers Should Make Decisions That Maximize Shareholder Value

This means making strategic decisions aimed at increasing the value of the firm.

If managers do not pursue value maximizing strategies, shareholder can take action through various corporate governance provisions

The Ten Principles of Finance

Principle 6: Transaction Costs, Taxes and
         Inflation are Your Enemies

- Transaction cost comes in many forms: brokerage commissions when you execute a trade, sales loads, 12b-1 and redemption fees when you purchase or sell a mutual fund and yearly asset management fees paid to a mutual fund, stockbroker or investment adviser
- Transaction costs and the effects of taxes and inflation can greatly reduce the real returns on your investments
- It should be every investor's mission to reduce her transaction costs to the lowest possible level

---

The Ten Principles of Finance

**Transaction Costs, Taxes and Inflation are
Your Enemies**

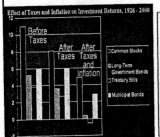

The long-term effect of taxes and inflation on investment returns for common stocks, long-term government bonds, Treasury Bills, and municipal bonds over 1926-1999 is shown in the graph

---

The Ten Principles of Finance

**Transaction Costs, Taxes and Inflation are
Your Enemies**

- As we observed in the graph, taxes can have a negative effect on investment performance and inflation decreases the real rate of return on the investment
- While inflation is beyond the control of the investor, investor can establish tax-advantaged accounts to accumulate retirement assets and can defer payment of taxes

The Ten Principles of Finance

<u>Principle 7:</u> Time and the Value of Money are Closely Related

- A dollar today is worth more than a dollar tomorrow
- To assess if an investment is good, you must be able to compare the value of money that you invest today with the value of the money that you expect to receive in the future and we use the process of compounding and discounting to make the comparison
- Compounding is the process of going from today's value, or present value (PV), to some expected but unknown future value (FV)

The Ten Principles of Finance

Time and the Value of Money are Closely Related

- Future value is the amount of money that an investment will grow to at some future date by earning interest at a certain rate

$$FV = PV * (1 + r)^n$$

- For example if you have a stock worth $10 that increases in value at the rate of 6% per year for five years, the value of stock at the end of five years

$$= \$10\,[(1+.06)^5] = \$13.38$$

The Ten Principles of Finance

Time and the Value of Money are Closely Related

- Discounting is the process of going from an expected future value to a present value
- The math underlying discounting and the calculation of present value is the exact flip side to compounding and future value
- Discount Factor = $1/(1 + r)^n$

- PV = FV * Discount Factor
- For example if you will be receiving $100 in 3 years and the discount rate is 10%, PV= $100 * [1/(1+.10)^3] = $75.13

The Ten Principles of Finance

<u>Principle 8</u>: Asset Allocation is a Very
          Important Decision

- To achieve the highest level of return for the amount of risk we can absorb, we should diversify our investment holdings over an array of assets classes
- The diversification process begins with asset allocation which is dividing investment funds among different asset classes
- The most basic asset classes are cash and short maturity deposits or securities, fixed income securities and bonds, and common stock

---

The Ten Principles of Finance

Asset Allocation is a Very Important Decision

The trade-off of risk and return that we discussed in Principle 1 also applies to asset classes, and is illustrated in the chart

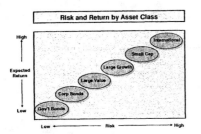

Risk and Return by Asset Class

The Ten Principles of Finance

Asset Allocation is a Very Important Decision

- Asset allocation is generally a personal decision which reflects beliefs about the anticipated risk and return of asset classes
- If you believe the stock market is going to crash, you should lower your stock allocation, shifting moneys to bonds or cash and alternatively if you believe that long-term interest rates are going to rise substantially, you should shift money from bonds into cash
- An element of market timing may be involved in asset allocation

The Ten Principles of Finance

Asset Allocation is a Very Important Decision

- Brinson study of investment performance of mutual funds and pension funds research showed that more than 90% of the variability in fund performance over time was attributable to asset allocation-meaning asset allocation is more important than the specific securities that are selected for investment
- Optimal asset allocation for an investor depends upon the risk/return profile of an investor—how much risk can he stomach when it comes to volatility and potential losses in his stock allocation and also depends upon where he is in his financial life cycle

The Ten Principles of Finance

Principle 9: Asset Diversification Will Reduce Risk

- To reduce the risk of your portfolio it is important to diversify your holdings
- Diversification means to spread your wealth among a number of different investments
- The goal of diversification is to invest in a group of assets that provides you with the best return possible given a level of risk

The Ten Principles of Finance

Asset Diversification Will Reduce Risk

- When making decisions affecting risk and return, consider the total amount of your assets—your career, house and all of your tangible and financial assets as being held in one portfolio, one pool
- For a first shot at diversification, try to separate your career assets from your investment assets
- Also since the goal of diversification is to reduce the downside risk of your asset base, avoid such things as investing in the stock of the company for which you work or investing in related industries

The Ten Principles of Finance

Asset Diversification Will Reduce Risk

- For financial assets it is important to know that the key to diversification and risk reduction is in the correlation of the returns of your assets
- Correlation is a statistic used in investing that measures the degree to which the movements of variables are related
- Correlation is measured on a scale of −1.0 to +1.0
- A correlation coefficient of 0.0 indicates no meaningful relationship between the two assets

---

The Ten Principles of Finance

Asset Diversification Will Reduce Risk

- A correlation coefficient of +1.0 between two stocks mean that when one stock is up 10%, the other stock will also go up 10% and correlation of −1.0 means that when one stock is up 5%, the other stock is down 5%
- Assets that are highly correlated offer less risk reduction from diversification than assets that are less correlated
- Diversification reduces the unsystematic risk of a portfolio. Unsystematic risk is specific to a company and Systematic risk represents the risk of the stock market

  Total Risk = Systematic Risk + Unsystematic Risk

The Ten Principles of Finance

Asset Diversification Will Reduce Risk

- Achieving the highest return for each level of risk is known as investing efficiently—investing on the <u>efficient frontier</u>
- Meir Statman study of randomly grouped portfolios of stocks of various sizes to determine the marginal amount of diversification achieved by adding additional stocks to a portfolio showed that just holding 10 stocks reduces volatility to an average of 23.93%, i.e. 50% less than average standard deviation of 49.24% for an individual stock.
- <u>Therefore, diversification greatly reduces risk with no cost.</u>

The Ten Principles of Finance

Asset Diversification Will Reduce Risk

The table below shows how many stocks your portfolio needs to hold to diversify risk

Number of Stocks in Portfolio	Average Std. Dev. of Annual Portfolio Returns	Ratio of Portfolio Std. Dev. of a Single Stock
1	49.24%	100%
10	23.93%	49%
50	20.20%	41%
100	19.69%	40%
300	19.34%	39%
500	19.27%	39%
1000	19.21%	39%

The Ten Principles of Finance

Asset Diversification Will Reduce Risk

- Diversification, while limiting your risk by spreading them over a larger number of securities, also limits the gains you would have received if you had concentrated your investments in a few stocks that turned out to be incredible winners
- To diversify intelligently apart from carefully investing career- oriented assets, house, and investments in your employer, divide the amount that you have allocated to your stock portfolio into twenty-5% increments and invest those increments in a combination of stocks and no-load mutual funds

The Ten Principles of Finance

Asset Diversification Will Reduce Risk

- If you are extremely bullish on a particular stock that you own, allow your relative portfolio percentage to increase, either through the appreciation in price of the stock over time or through an additional purchase, to a maximum 10% of your equity portfolio
- Any portion over 10% should be sold when you rebalance your equity portfolio, which should be performed on an annual basis
- You could also combine the proportions of individual stocks and mutual funds to achieve your desired stock asset class allocation

The Ten Principles of Finance

Principle 10: An Asset Pricing Model Should be Used to Value Investments

- The Capital Asset Pricing Model (CAPM) is a simple model that estimates the rate of return an investor should expect to receive on a risky asset
- In valuation, its principal purpose is to determine the discount rate to use when valuing an asset
- CAPM states that the expected return of a risky asset, $E(R_i)$, such as a common stock, is equal to the return on the risk-free asset (R_f) plus a risk premium

The Ten Principles of Finance

An Asset Pricing Model Should be Used to Value Investments

$$\text{Expected Return} = \text{Risk-Free Rate} + \text{Risk Premium}$$
$$E(R_i) = R_f + \beta_i * [E(R_m) - R_f]$$

- The risk-free rate (R_f) that we use for valuation is the rate on the long-term (10-year) Treasury bond
- The risk premium is a function of two factors: the stock's beta (β_i), and the market risk premium, which is the expected return on the overall stock market (R_m) minus the risk free rate: $[E(R_m) - R_f]$

The Ten Principles of Finance

Principle 10: An Asset Pricing Model Should be Used to Value Investments

- The Capital Asset Pricing Model (CAPM) is a simple model that estimates the rate of return an investor should expect to receive on a risky asset
- In valuation, its principal purpose is to determine the discount rate to use when valuing an asset
- CAPM states that the expected return of a risky asset, $E(R_i)$, such as a common stock, is equal to the return on the risk-free asset (R_f) plus a risk premium

The Ten Principles of Finance
Relating to Valuation

Principle 10: An Asset Pricing Model Should be Used to Value Investments

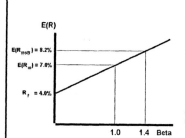

If the stock market prices stocks in the manner consistent with the Capital Asset Pricing Model, the expected return on each stock should fall on the diagonal risk/return line shown in the chart

The Ten Principles of Finance
Relating to Valuation

An Asset Pricing Model Should be Used to Value Investments

CAPM Example: Suppose the risk free rate is 4% and an expected return on the stock market is 6% and if beta of XYZ Inc is 1.2 calculate the expected return of XYZ Inc.

$$E(R_{xyz}) = R_f + ß_i * [E(R_m) - R_f]$$
$$E(R_{xyz}) = 4\% + 1.2 (6\% - 4\%)$$
$$= 6.4\%$$

CAPM is a very simple yet powerful way to estimate the cost of equity, which is usually the most significant component of a company's weighted cost of capital

CAPM versus Beta for Stocks

Expected Return

IBM

AT&T

Micro -soft

USX

Beta

Chapter 3

Corporate Finance, Creating Shareholder Value, and and Corporate Governance

---

Corporate Finance, Creating Shareholder Value, and and Corporate Governance

The objectives of the session include:

(1) Understand the role of finance in business and the economy;
(2) Appreciate the evolving role of the finance function in business;
(3) Review the responsibilities of the chief financial officer (CFO);
(4) Develop a knowledge of the alternative legal structures for a firm;
(5) Discuss the principal goal of a publicly-held corporation;
(6) Define how firms create shareholder value;
(7) Debate the claims of shareholders versus stakeholders;
(8) Examine corporate governance and the agency problem;
(9) Trace the recent changes in corporate governance; and
(10) Discuss global models of corporate

Financial Facts of the Day

The Largest Companies in the World

ale	Profit$

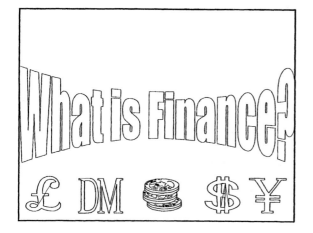

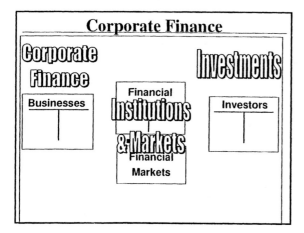

The New Corporate Finance and Capital Markets

1. The New Corporate Finance

2. The New Role of the CFO and the Evolving Finance Function

3. The Primary Issues in Corporate Finance

4. The Basic Tenets of Corporate Finance

The Finance Function

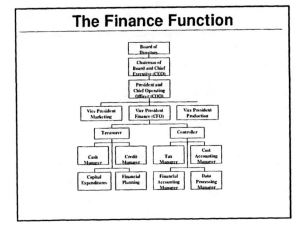

Board of Directors
Chairman of Board and Chief Executive (CEO)
President and Chief Operating Officer (COO)
Vice President Marketing | Vice President Finance (CFO) | Vice President Production
Treasurer | Controller
Cash Manager | Credit Manager | Tax Manager | Cost Accounting Manager
Capital Expenditures | Financial Planning | Financial Accounting Manager | Data Processing Manager

The Finance Function

Treasurer

Financial Planning
Capital Budgets
S-T and L-T Capital
Requirements
Cash Management
 and Working Capital

Controller

Financial Statements
 and Reports
Financial Systems
Operating Budgets
Audits
Taxes

The New Corporate Finance

1. The Finance Environment

2. Elements of the New
   Financial Environment

3. Advances in Finance

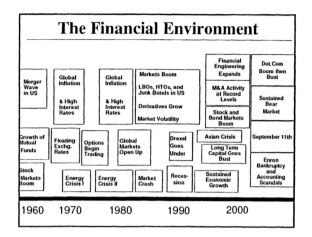

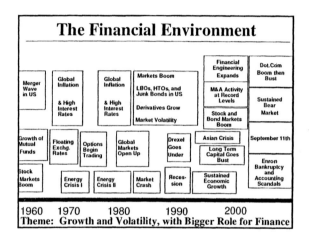

The New Corporate Finance
Elements of the New Environment

**Advances in Information, Systems,
and Telecommunications Technologies**

Growth in Trade and Direct Investment

Deregulation and Growth of Global Markets

Greater Economic Volatility and Risk

New Complex Financial Instruments

Institutionalization of Markets

New Markets and Financial Institutions

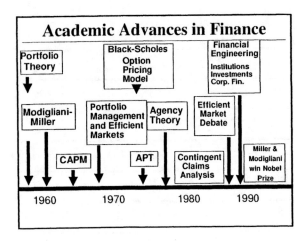

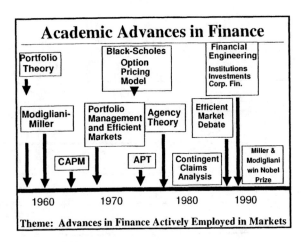

Theme: **Advances in Finance Actively Employed in Markets**

The CFO as Financial Engineer

Traditional Roles

■ **Controller Functions** – Planning and Control, Systems, Financial Statements and Reports, Taxes, Budgets

■ **Treasury Functions** – Cash and Working Capital Management, Capital Budgets, L-T Financial Planning

Expanded Roles

■ **Corporate Strategist** – Assist in Strategy Formulation

■ **Financing and Capitalization** – Insure that Capital is Available to Fund Strategic Plan

■ **Risk Management** – Hedge Risks (Currency, Commodity, Financial) in Markets When Appropriate

■ **Growth and Acquisitions** – Provide for Growth Opportunities

Matthew J. Hart

Winner In Category Of <u>Deal-Making And Integration</u>

$3.7 Billion Acquisition Of Promus Hotels Made Hilton One Of The Biggest Hotel Chains In Country

Revenue Rose To $3.5 Billion

Success Of Merger Attributed To His <u>Ability To Integrate Companies</u> Despite Differences In How They Operate

(H) Hilton

Andy Bryant

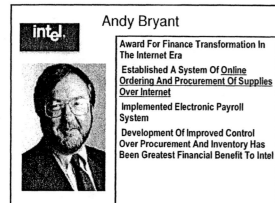

intel.

Award For Finance Transformation In The Internet Era

Established A System Of <u>Online Ordering And Procurement Of Supplies Over Internet</u>

Implemented Electronic Payroll System

Development Of Improved Control Over Procurement And Inventory Has Been Greatest Financial Benefit To Intel

Strategic Financial Management

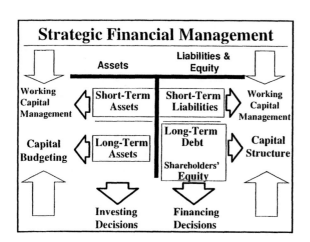

25

Strategic Financial Management

Assets	Liabilities & Equity
Current Assets Cash Accounts Receivable Inventories	**Current Liabilities** S-T Loans Accounts Payable

Working Capital Management
Managing Short Term Financial Position of the Firm

Strategic Financial Management

Assets	Liabilities & Equity
Long-Term Assets Property, Plant. & Equipment	

Capital Budgeting
Managing Investments in Long-Term Assets

Strategic Financial Management

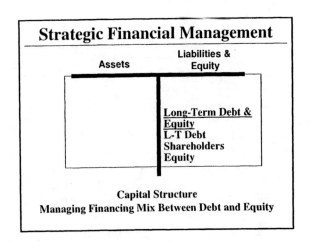

Assets	Liabilities & Equity
	Long-Term Debt & Equity L-T Debt Shareholders Equity

Capital Structure
Managing Financing Mix Between Debt and Equity

New Corporate Finance and Capital Markets
Key Learning Points

1. Corporate Finance, its Evolving Function, and the CFO

2. The New Environment of Corporate Finance

3. The Primary Issues in Corporate Finance

4. The Basic Tenets of Corporate Finance

5. The Financial Tool Box

BA 301
Finance and Financial Services
Assignment for Next Class

→ Reading: Creating Shareholder Value and Corporate Governance

→ AMP Case Study

→ End of Chapter Terms and Questions

New Corporate Finance and Capital Markets
Exam Questions

1. Finance vs. Accounting Treasurer vs. Controller

2. Finance in the New Environment

3. The New Role of Finance

4. Strategic Financial Decisions

5. The Basic Tenets of Corporate Finance

6. The Financial Toolbox

Creating Shareholder Value and Corporate Governance

_____

_____

_____

_____

_____

_____

_____

Creating Shareholder Value - What does it Mean?

_____

_____

_____

_____

_____

_____

Market Capitalization

⊙ TARGET

■ Market Cap – The Aggregate Market Value of a Company

Market Cap =

# of Shares * Price Per Share

■ Why is it Important?

_____

_____

_____

_____

_____

_____

Target Corp.

Target Corporation reflects our belief that we maximize shareholder value by leveraging our resources across the organization. Though we operate three distinct retail segments, we strengthen our overall competitive position and increase our efficiency and profitability by capturing the synergies inherent in our business and pursuing a singular corporate vision.

Target Corporation is committed to delivering superior returns to our shareholders. Over the past five years, we have generated a total annualized return of 44 percent, well above the 18 percent return for the S&P 500 and the 24 percent return generated by the S&P Retail Index.

Papa Johns

Customers
Papa John's will create superior brand loyalty, i.e. "raving fans", through (a) authentic, superior-quality products, (b) legendary customer service and (c) exceptional community service.

Team Members
People are our most important asset. Papa John's will provide clear, consistent, strategic leadership and career opportunities for Team Members who exhibit passion toward their work, (b) uphold our Core Values, (c) take pride of ownership in building the long-term value of the Papa John's brand and (d) have ethical business practices.

Franchisees
We will partner with our franchisees to create continued opportunity for outstanding financial returns to those franchisees who adhere to Papa John's proven Core Values and systems, (b) exhibit passion in running their businesses and (c) take pride of ownership in building the long-term value of the Papa John's brand.

Shareholders
We will produce superior long-term value for our shareholders.

Verizon

Verizon is Committed to Steady, Long-Term Growth in Shareholder Value

- → Aggressive Top Line Growth
- → Productivity Improvement
- → Effective Investment Allocation
- → Balanced Funding Strategy

Income Statement	Balance Sheet	
	Assets	Liabilities & Equity
Sales ➢ Aggressive Top Line Growth	Make Good Investments	Effective Use of Debt And Equity Financing
➢ Productivity Improvement		
Net Income	➢ Effective Investment Allocation	➢ Balanced Funding Strategy

Statement of Corporate Purpose
Oren Harari, "You're not in Business to Make a Profit"

"Many Managers in the U.S. Still Operate Under the Twin Fictions That Their Most Important Stakeholders are Shareholders, and That Their Primary Purpose in Management is to Enhance Shareholder Value. From both an Operational and Strategic Perspective, This is Dead Wrong. <u>A Business does not Exist for the Benefit of Investors, Nor Should it be Run Under That Premise.</u>"

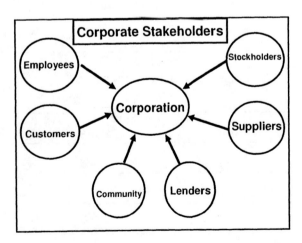

Corporate Stakeholders

Employees → Corporation
Stockholders → Corporation
Customers → Corporation
Suppliers → Corporation
Community → Corporation
Lenders → Corporation

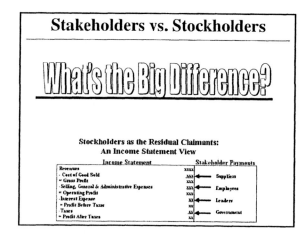

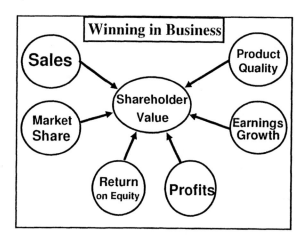

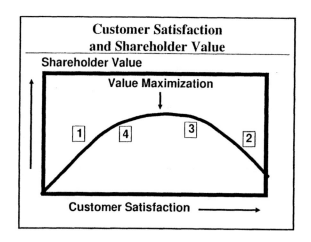

Creating Shareholder Value

How does Management Create Shareholder Value?

Asset Management   Liability Management

Avenues of Shareholder Value Creation

Financial Management

Asset Management   Liability Management

Goal	Goal
To Allocate Capital to Investments Offering the Highest Risk-Adjusted Returns	To Minimize the Cost of Capital
To Minimize the Amount of Capital Required to Achieve the Company's Objective	o Financial Engineering - Debt/Equity Management - Financial Innovation - Strategic Risk Management
o Working Capital Management	
o Fixed Capital Management	To Enhance Performance
	o Ownership Structure

Business Organizational Forms

1. Sole Proprietorships

2. Partnerships

3. Corporations

Form	Sole Proprietorship	Partnership	Corporation
Ease of Formation	Easy	More Difficult	Difficult – Separate Legal Entity
Tax	Profits Taxed as Income	Profits Taxed as Income	Double Taxed – Corp. & Individual
Ease of Transfer	Difficult	More Difficult	Easy
Liability	Liable for Liabilities	Liable for Liabilities	Limited Liability
Ability to Raise Capital	Difficult	Difficult	Relatively Easy

Corporate Governance

◆ **A Corporation is**
  – **Legal entity which serves as a nexus of contracts whereby individuals contract with each other in the name of the corporation**
  – **is dynamic and not a creature of the state**

◆ **Brief History**
  – **State chartering process**
  – **Not always dominant organizational form**
  – **Advantages of the corporate organizational form**
    – **Limited liability**
    – **Access to capital**
    – **Liquidity for owners**

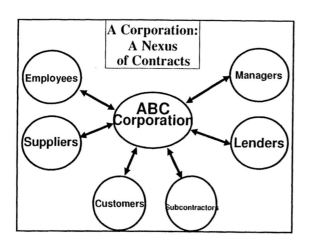

A Corporation: A Nexus of Contracts

What is Corporate Governance?

**Corporation Governance involves
the Rules and Procedures that
Prescribe how Shareholders (the Owners)
Insure that Managers are Acting
to Enhance the Value of a Corporation**

Corporate Governance:
The Agency Problem

- ◆ **Separation of Ownership and Control**
  - – Berle & Means (1932) - *The Modern Corporation and Private Property*
  - – Asset Ownership Versus Control

- ◆ **The Core Issue - The Agency Problem**
  - – Managers are Agents of Stockholders
  - – Managers May Act in Own Self Interest if Consequences are Not Severe Enough

---

The Agency Problem
Separation of Ownership and Control

Ownership

Stockholders

The Agency Problem

Control

Management

Corporate Control

Corporate Control Mechanisms Are Designed to Insure that Management Acts in Shareholder Interests

- ◆ **Internal Control Mechanisms**
  - Board of Directors
  - Audited Financial Statements
  - Stock Value–Based Compensation
  - Stock Ownership Interest

- ◆ **External Control Mechanisms**
  - Managerial Labor Market
  - Market for Corporate Control
  - Shareholder Activism

The US Board of Directors Model

Shareholders

▼ ▼ ▼

▼ ▼ ▼

Management

Corporate Takeovers in the 1980s: The Failure of Internal Control Mechanisms

- ◆ **Diffusion of Stock Ownership**
  - Reduced Stockholder influence in Corporate Governance Issues
  - Costs of Monitoring Management Performance Too High

- ◆ **Unfair Corporate Voting Procedures – Board Members & Management**
  - Proxy Solicitation Procedures
  - Access to Stockholders
  - Nonconfidential voting

- ◆ **Low Degree of Managerial Stock Ownership**

35

Other People's Money

Questions

◆ Who are Gregory Peck and Danny Devito Talking to?

◆ Who has Replaced the Danny Devitos in the Public's Eye?

Corporate Governance
Since the 1980s

◆ The Board's Role is Changing
  - CEOs Fired for Poor Performance

◆ Debate over Executive Compensation
  - Management Pay Versus Performance
  - Issue of Management Stock Ownership

◆ Institutional Investors are Becoming More Involved in Corporate Governance Issues
  - Proxy Rules are Being Changed (Voting)
  - Shareholders Communications Permitted
  - The Demise of Managerial Defense Mechanisms (e.g., Poison Pills)
  - The Move to Shared Governance

Shareholder Activism and Stock Returns

The Council of Institutional Investors Annually Places Poorly Performing Companies on its 'Focus List'

Stock and Profit Performance for Laggard Companies Before and After Being Added to the CII Focus List

Cumulative Stock Performance

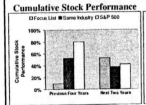

Return on Assets

Source: Opler and Sokobin

CII Core Board Policies
to Maintain Independence

1. Directors should be elected annually with confidential voting;
2. At least two-thirds of the corporation's directors should be from outside the corporation to prevent biased opinions;
3. Shareholders should have adequate information regarding director backgrounds and status as independent or associated with the corporation;
4. All members of oversight committees should be independent directs to prevent biased opinions; and
5. A majority vote from common shareholders should be required to pass any major corporate decision.

Corporate Governance
Alternative Models

◆ **Anglo-American Model**
  - Minority Shareholders with Board
  - Problems Led to 1980s Takeovers

◆ **Japan-Germany Dedicated Capital Model**
  - Large Equity Holders Provide Oversight
  - Very Few Takeovers

◆ **Rest of World Majority Owner Model**
  - Majority Equity Owner Oversees Management

Corporate Governance
Alternative Models

Anglo-American Model

Characteristics:
Primarily Minority Shareholders
Board of Directors Elected to Represent Shareholders Interests
Fluid Capital Model – Capital Flows to Firms with Best Prospects to Create Shareholder Value

Corporate Governance
Alternative Models

Japan		Germany	
Kierstu	O	Hausbank	

mitsubishi

Deutsche Bank

DB is a Major Provider of Debt
And Equity Capital and is on
the Supervisory Board

DAIMLERCHRYSLER

Companies in Business Together that
Own Each Other's Common Stock

Characteristics:
Dedicated Capital – Equity not Sold – Governance Issues

Corporate Governance
Alternative Models
Rest of World Majority Owner Model
Majority Equity Owner Oversees Management

Characteristics:
Company Managed According to the Interests
Of the Majority Owner

The Crisis in Corporate Governance

◆ Executive Compensation

◆ The Board of Directors

◆ Accounting and Auditing

◆ Wall Street Analysts

◆ The Justice Department
  and the SEC:
  Enforcement and
   Transparency

◆ Leadership

The Crisis in Corporate Governance
Executive Compensation

Bragging Rights

NEW YORK - Larry Ellison, Oracle's flamboyant chief executive, earned a stunning $706 million in total compensation last year. Assuming a 40-hour workweek, that works out to nearly $340,000 an hour. Total one-year return for Oracle's shareholders in 2001? Minus 25%.

Here's a look at the ten top-earning chief executives in 2001, based on early filings. We also show their one-year total return to shareholders. The pay figures are drawn from 140 Forbes 500 companies that had filed data as of early March. On average, the top ten chief executives earned $126 million, while returning less than 1% to their shareholders.

We measure total compensation by summing up salary and bonuses, realized gains in stock options, vested stock grants and "other compensation," such as company-paid insurance and perks. Company total returns are based on March 7's close.

SOURCE: http://www.forbes.com/2002/03/19/0319wrap.html

Executive Compensation

The Crisis in Corporate Governance
Auditing and Accounting

Global Crossing

Conflicts of Interest

Joseph Perrone, Executive VP of finance at Global Crossing (GC), previously headed the Arthur Anderson team responsible for auditing GC's books

At GC, Perrone was in charge of overseeing the way that GC booked revenue from network capacity swaps

Those accounting methods are under investigation by the SEC and FBI

Source: Jubak, Jim. "8 Companies Whose Board Need a Scare" MSN/Money. 2 April 2002

The Crisis in Corporate Governance
The Board of Directors

The Fall of Tyco

The Board of Directors

The Fall of Tyco   ◇ Click on the links to see the relevant articles

Jan. 7 Newsletter renews worries about accounting

Jan. 16 Posts negative cash flow, gives gloomy outlook

Jan. 23 Sets plan to break into four companies

Feb. 4 Confirms spending $8 bil on 700 unannounced acquisitions

Feb. 6 May face trouble selling short-term debt

April 26 Abandons plans for breakup

June 3 Kozlowski resigns

Dec. Jan 2002 Feb. March April May

Source: Dow Jones Interactive, WSJ Online research

Go to The Rise of Tyco

Source: *The Wall Street Journal*, 10 June 2002.

The Issues

Excessive Executive Compensation

Insider Financial Transactions

Aggressive Acquisitions

Questionable Accounting Practices

Adelphia Communications

Adelphia

The Board of Directors

Where's the Board of Directors?

Guaranteed loans of $2.3 Billion to Rigas family who founded and own most of Adelphia

Adelphia CFO said that the loan was secured by assets that would normally be able to secure no more than $700 Million

Debt, which Adelphia was liable for, did not appear on balance sheet

CFO: Timothy Rigas, son of then CEO John Rigas

Source: Jubak, Jim. "8 Companies Whose Board Need a Scare" MSN/Money. 2 April 2002

The Crisis in Corporate Governance
Wall Street Analysts

Analyst's Contracts Tell All
Wall Street Analysts

DOING DOUBLE DUTY?

Copies of job-offer letters' from Donaldson, Lufkin & Jenrette and Credit Suisse First Boston to candidates for research-analyst positions show that Wall Street analysts are paid, in part, for investment-banking business they helped generate. Below, with personal data blacked out.

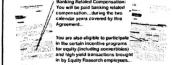

Banking Related Compensation: You will be paid banking related compensation...during the two calendar years covered by this Agreement...

You are also eligible to participate in the certain incentive programs for equity (including convertibles) and high yield transactions brought in by Equity Research employees...

"We're just beginning to see massive evidence that analysts' research for years have been tainted by employment contracts that directly compensate them"

Eliot Spitzer, New York State Attorney General

Source: Gasparino, Charles. *The Wall Street Journal.* 6 May 2002.

The Crisis in Corporate Governance
The Justice Department
& the SEC

Al Dunlap & Sunbeam

The notorious Al "Chainsaw" Dunlap, accused of zealously fabricating Sunbeam's financial statements when he was chief executive, is facing only civil, not criminal, charges. The SEC charged that Dunlap and his minions made use of every accounting fraud in the book, from "channel stuffing" to "cookie jar reserves." The case is now in the discovery phase of trial and likely to be settled: he has denied wrongdoing. (Earlier Chainsaw rid himself of a class-action shareholder suit for $15 million, without admitting culpability.) Whatever the current trial's outcome, Dunlap will still come out well ahead. Sunbeam, now under bankruptcy protection, gave him $12.7 million in stock and salary during 1998 alone. And if worse comes to worst, he can always tap the stash he got from the sale of the disemboweled Scott Paper to Kimberly-Clark, which by Dunlap's own estimate netted him a $100 million bonanza.

Sunbeam investors, naturally, didn't fare as well. When the fraud was discovered internally, the company was forced to restate its earnings, slashing half the reported profits from fiscal 1997. After that embarrassment, Sunbeam shares fell from $52 to $7 in just six months--a loss of $3.8 billion in market cap. Sound familiar?

The auditor in that case, you'll recall, was Arthur Andersen, which paid $110 million to settle a civil action. According to an SEC release in May, an Andersen partner authorized unqualified audit opinions even though "he was aware of many of the company's accounting improprieties and disclosure failures." The opinions were false and misleading. But nobody is going to jail.

At Waste Management, yet another Andersen client, income reported over six years was overstated by $1.4 billion. Andersen coughed up $220 million to shareholders to wipe its hands clean. The auditor, agreeing to the SEC's first antifraud injunction against a major firm in more than 20 years, also paid a $7 million fine to close the complaint. Three partners were assessed fines, ranging from $30,000 to $50,000, as well.

Financial Ethics

Finally, a price must be exacted for failure to do the right thing. "We had Sunbeam, Waste Management (WMI), and Cendant--and I don't think anybody has gone to jail yet, and I don't know why," says Philip B. Livingston, president of Financial Executives International, a professional group of finance managers. "When the SEC and the Justice Dept. get their act together and start sending some CFOs and CEOs to jail, you'll see a real wake-up call."

Creating Shareholder Value
and Corporate Governance

Key Learning Points

1. Creating Shareholder Value

2. Avenues of Value Creation

3. Corporate Form of Organization

4. The Agency Problem and Corporate Control

5. Governance in the 80's, 90's, and 00's

6. Global Corporate Governance

7. The Crisis in Corporate Governance

7. Gekko, Devito, and AMP

Strategic Financial Management

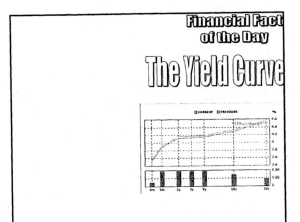

Strategic Financial Management

This module covers the primary areas of strategic financial management. The objectives of the session include:

(1) Illustrating short-term financial strategy in the the form of working capital management;

(2) Assessing capital budgeting in the context of a firm;

(3) Evaluating the role of capital structure and dividend policy in long-term financial strategy.

Strategic Financial Management

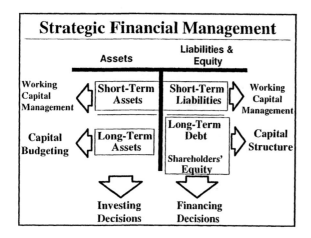

Assets | Liabilities & Equity

Working Capital Management ⇐ **Short-Term Assets** | **Short-Term Liabilities** ⇒ Working Capital Management

Capital Budgeting ⇐ **Long-Term Assets** | **Long-Term Debt** / **Shareholders' Equity** ⇒ Capital Structure

⇓ Investing Decisions | ⇓ Financing Decisions

Strategic Financial Management

Assets | Liabilities & Equity

Current Assets
Cash
Accounts Receivable
Inventories

Current Liabilities
S-T Loans
Accounts Payable

Working Capital Management
Managing Short Term Financial Position of the Firm

Working Capital Management

1. Old Paradigm/New Paradigm

2. The Costs of Holding Current Assets

3. The Short-Term Operating Cycle and the Cash Conversion Cycle

4. Financing Short-Term Assets

Working Capital Management

→ **Old Paradigm**
  - Working Capital
    is Good (liquidity)
  - Measure:
    Current Ratio of 2.0

→ **New Paradigm**
  - Working Capital is Bad
  - Reflects Poor Planning
  - Use of Funds
  - Measure: W/C / Sales

The Costs of Holding Current Assets

Costs of Holding Current Assets

Carrying Costs
Capital Costs - Cost of Funds Invested
Warehousing - Inventory
Insurance - Inventory
Bad Credit - Accounts Receivable

Shortage Costs
Stock Outs - Run out of Inventory
Sales - Tight Credit Limits Sales

The Costs of Maintaining Inventory

Inventory Costs as a Percent of Inventory

Warehousing Costs	
Space	
Utilities	
Taxes	
Equipment	0.60
People	
Fringe Benefits	
Spoilage and Obsolescence	0.30
Computer and Financial Systems to Monitor Inventories	0.20
Insurance	0.05
Cost of Capital	1.00
Total Cost	2.15

Biggest Costs:
Warehousing & Capital

Old Paradigm:
Excess Inventory adds
Value to Customers

New Paradigm:
Reduce Inventory by
Changing Processes and
Working with Suppliers

Short-Term Operating Cycle

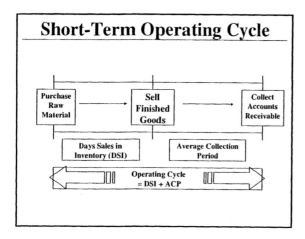

Purchasing and Accounts Payable

→ **Old Paradigm**
- The Supplier is an Adversary
- Key Issue: Lower Prices

→ **New Paradigm**
- Timeliness of Delivery May be More Important Than Price
- Good Purchasing Includes Terms, Quality, and Delivery
- The Cost of not Taking Discounts is Prohibitive

Working Capital Management

Assets	Liabilities
Cash Marketable Securities	Bank Loans
Accounts Receivable *Credit Policy* *- A/R Turn - ACP (Days Sales Outstanding)*	Accounts Payable *Payables Policy* *- Payables Turn - (Days Payables Outstanding)*
Inventories *Inventory Policy* *- Inv Turn - (Days in Inventory)*	
	Accrued Expenses
Total Current Assets	Total Current Liabilities

Supplier Credit and the CCC
What is the Cash Conversion Cycle?

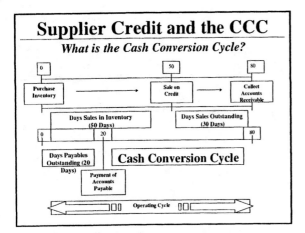

CCC – The Dell Example

■ 1993 – Inventories and Receivables Were Increasing Faster Than Revenues At Dell Computer

■ CFO Tom Meredith Developed the CCC Metric to Measure Dell's Progress In Converting Sales to Cash

■ Improved Dell's CCC From 46 In 1995 to –20 In 1999

Calculating the CCC

CCC	=	DSO	+	DSI	-	DPO

■ CCC = Cash Conversion Cycle

■ DSO = Days Sales Outstanding or Average Collection Period

■ DSI = Days Sales In Inventory

■ DPO = Days Payables Outstanding or Average Payables Period

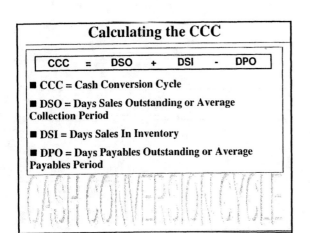

Calculating the CCC

■ Days Sales Outstanding or Average Collection Period:

■ Days Sales In Inventory:

■ Days Payables Outstanding or Average Payables Period:

Strategic Financial Management

Metric	1995	1997	1999
Days Sales Outstanding	42	37	38
Days Sales in Inventory	37	13	6
Days Payables Outstanding	33	54	64
Cash Conversion Cycle	46	-5	-20

Improving the Firm's CCC

■ Firms Can Do the Following to Improve Their Cash Conversion Cycle:

■ Expedite Collections

■ Increase Inventory Turnover (E.g., JIT Technique)

■ Lengthen Payables Period

Financing Short-Term Assets

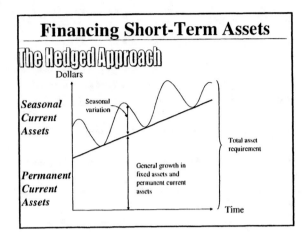

Strategic Financial Management

Capital Budgeting
Definition

The Capital Allocation Process Involves Current Outlays of Funds in Anticipation of Generating Future Cash Flows

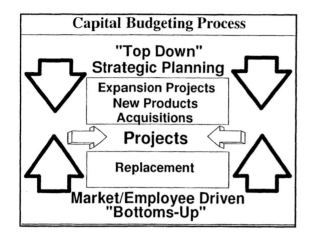

Capital Budgeting Process

"Top Down"
Strategic Planning

Expansion Projects
New Products
Acquisitions

Projects

Replacement

Market/Employee Driven
"Bottoms-Up"

◆ **Planning and Budgeting**
  - Identifying Potential
    Projects in the Strategic
    Planning Process

◆ **Evaluation**
  - Projecting Cash Flows and
    Applying Capital
    Budgeting Techniques

◆ **Post-Completion Reviews**
  - Compare Actual Versus
    Projected Results

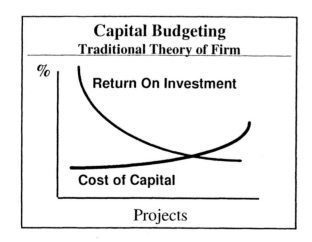

Capital Budgeting
Traditional Theory of Firm

%

Return On Investment

Cost of Capital

Projects

Capital Investment and Market Values
Investment Decisions and Stock Prices

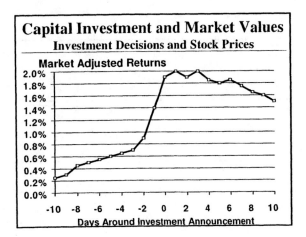

Market Adjusted Returns

Days Around Investment Announcement

Capital Budgeting

→ **Types of Corporate Investment Decisions**
- **Replacement**
- **Expansion**

Capital Budgeting
Good Investments?

→ **Microsoft Spent over $500 M Developing Windows 95/98**

→ **Boeing has Spent over $ 5 B Developing the 777**

→ **The Alaskian Pipeline Cost over $15 B**

→ **Disney Spent $50M Making** *The Lion King*

Capital Budgeting
Bad Investments?

→ GM Invested Invested Over $101 Billion During the 1980s on Company Infrastructure

→ IBM Spent over $25 B on R&D During the 1985-1990 Period

→ RJR-Nabisco Spent $100 M on a Smokeless Cigarette Which was Never Marketed

→ EuroDisney Cost Over $4 B

Categories of Investments
Expansion

MOTOROLA

The Iridium Project

Motorola, Along With Over 50 Global Partners, Spent Over $5B to Launch and Deploy 66 Satelites to Provide Cellular Communications Worldwide

Capital Budgeting

→ The Returns of a College Education

Capital Budgeting
The Returns of a College Education

➔ **Cost**
- Avg. Cost - $22,000/Year

➔ **Salary Differentials**
- College Grads Earn 89% More Than Non-Grads, Up From 49% More in 1979

➔ **Return**
- Assuming 75% of Difference Due to Education, You Earn an 11% Return

Strategic Financial Management

Assets   Liabilities & Equity

Long-Term Debt & Equity
L-T Debt
Shareholders
Equity

Capital Structure
Managing Financing Mix Between Debt and Equity

Capital Structure and Firm Valuation

➔ Companies Need Capital to Grow

➔ For a Typical Firm, 70% is Generated Internally from Operations

➔ The Remainder Must be Raised from the Markets

➔ Key Issue:
Should it be Debt or Equity

Using Debt to Raise Capital

◆ **Advantages**
  - **Interest is Tax Deductible**

◆ **Disadvantages**
  - **Incurr a Fixed Financing Obligation in the Form of Interest and Principle Payments Which can Lead to Financial Distress**

Using Common Stock to Raise Capital

◆ **Advantages**
  - **No Fixed Financing Obligation**

◆ **Disadvantages**
  - **Dilutes Ownership Interests**
  - **Higher Cost Than Debt**

Capital Structure Policies

	Debt %	Equity %	# Times Interest Earned	Financial Strength	Sales Growth	Stock Risk 1-Low--5-High
Microsoft	0	100	nmf	A++	12%	4
Intel	3	97	30X	A++	6%	5
Coca-Cola	20	80	21X	A++	6%	2
Merck	22	78	22X	A++	12%	3
WalMart	32	68	10X	A++	12%	3
The Walt Disney Company	35	65	6X	A	5%	4
McDonald's	47	53	7X	A++	5%	3
Consolidated Edison	50	50	4X	A++	2%	1
Hilton Hotels	72	28	2X	C++	2%	4
AMR Corp.	83	17	2X	C	NMF	5
Nextel Communications	86	14	2X	C+	6%	5

Data Source: *Value Line Investment Survey*.

Capital Structure and Firm Valuation

◆ **Capital Structure Ratios of US Industry**
  - High Degrees of Leverage
    Public Utilities, Publishing, Broadcasting, Real Estate, Transportation
  - Low Degrees of Leverage
    Computer Software, Drugs

◆ **Capital Structure Policies**

Capital Structure and Firm Valuation

The Capital Structure Puzzle

◆ **Does An Optimal Capital Structure Exist?**
  - Can the Use of Debt Financing Increase Firm Value?

◆ **The Static Trade-Off Theory**
  - Trade–Off Between Tax Savings and Financial Distress Costs of Debt

---

Optimal Capital Structure

The Impact of The Tax Deductibility of Interest

%

K$_e$

Cost Of Capital

Cost of Capital

Debt/Assets

Optimal Capital Structure

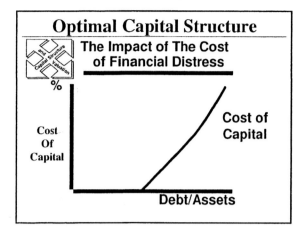

The Impact of The Cost of Financial Distress

Cost Of Capital (%)

Cost of Capital

Debt/Assets

Financial Distress Costs of Debt

→ **Direct Costs - Bankruptcy**
   - **Studies Indicate that Legal and Administrative Costs are 5% of Firm Value**

→ **Indirect Costs**
   - **Costs Occurred When Problems Associated With Meeting Debt Payments Impair Firm Operations (Employees Leave, Programs Dropped, Operations Disrupted)**

The Probability of Financial Distress

■ **Determinants of Business Risk:**

■ **Firm's Cost Structure**

■ **Demand Stability**

■ **Competition**

■ **Price Fluctuations**

■ **Firm Size and Diversification**

■ **Stage In Industry Life Cycle**

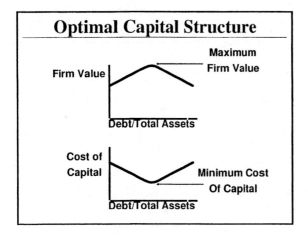

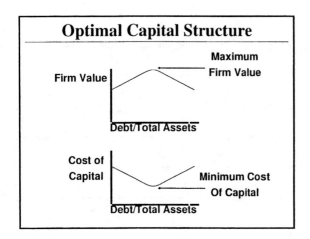

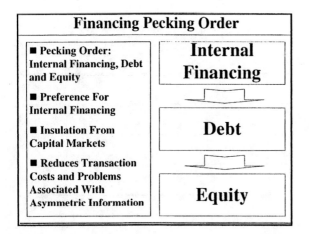

The Cost of Capital
Target vs Walmart

Source	($)	Ratio	After-Tax Cost	Weighted Cost
Debt				
Common Stock				

Overall Cost of Capital

The Cost of Capital
Target vs Walmart

Source	($)	Ratio	After-Tax Cost	Weighted Cost
Debt				
Common Stock				

Overall Cost of Capital

Other Factors Influencing Financial Structure

- Need to Preserve Financial Flexibility Limit Use of Debt

- With More Debt, Firms Become Easy Prey to Competitors

- Need For Financial Reserves Valuable to Firms With Limited Access to Financial Markets

- Firms With Growth Options Should Maintain Large Financial Reserves

Capital Structure and Firm Valuation
The Determinants of Corporate Debt Levels

◆ The Tax–Shield Effect of Interest Payments

◆ The Relative Degree of Business Risk
  - The Probability and Cost of Incurring
    Financial Distress

◆ The Nature of a Firm's Assets and Value
  - Tangible Assets and Value
  - Intangible Assets and Value

◆ Financial Slack
  - Investment Opportunities
  - Growth

◆ The Ownership Structure of the Firm

Dividend Policy and Firm Valuation

Dividend Changes and Stock Prices
Dividend Increases and Decreases

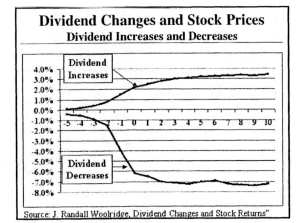

Source: J. Randall Woolridge, Dividend Changes and Stock Returns"

Dividend Payout Policies

	Stock Price	2003 Dividend	Dividend Yield	2003 Earnings	Dividend Payout Ratio	Projected Dividend Growth
Microsoft	$ 25	$ 0.08	0.3%	$ 0.95	8.4%	25%
Intel	$ 16	$ 0.10	0.6%	$ 0.60	16.7%	10%
Coca-Cola	$ 40	$ 0.84	2.1%	$ 1.92	43.8%	8%
Merck	$ 60	$ 1.46	2.4%	$ 3.45	42.3%	8%
WalMart	$ 48	$ 0.32	0.7%	$ 2.05	15.6%	12%
The Walt Disney Company	$ 16	$ 0.21	1.3%	$ 0.70	30.0%	0%
McDonald's	$ 13	$ 0.26	2.0%	$ 1.45	17.9%	5%
Consolidated Edison	$ 40	$ 2.36	5.9%	$ 3.10	76.1%	1%
Hilton Hotels	$ 12	$ 0.08	0.7%	$ 0.45	17.8%	0%
AMR Corp.	$ 2	$ -	NMF	$ (7.50)	0%	Nil
Nextel Communications	$ 12	$ -	NMF	$ 0.70	0%	Nil

Data Source: *Value Line Investment Survey*.

Dividend Payout Policies

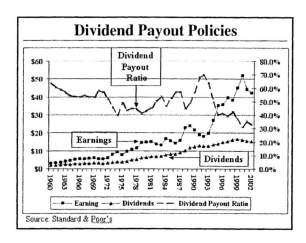

Source: Standard & Poor's

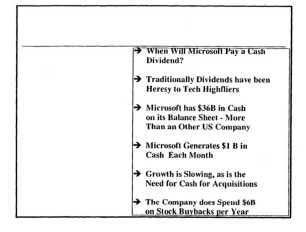

→ When Will Microsoft Pay a Cash Dividend?

→ Traditionally Dividends have been Heresy to Tech Highfliers

→ Microsoft has $36B in Cash on its Balance Sheet - More Than an Other US Company

→ Microsoft Generates $1 B in Cash Each Month

→ Growth is Slowing, as is the Need for Cash for Acquisitions

→ The Company does Spend $6B on Stock Buybacks per Year

Dividend Policy and Firm Value
Summary Points

→ A Firm's Dividend Policy is Primarily a Function of It's Investment Opportunities

→ Announcements of Dividend Changes are Usually Accompanied with Like Changes in Stock Prices

→ Stock Prices React to Dividend Change Announcements due to the Information in the Announcements, Not Due to the Dividend Itself

Financial Statements, Analysis, and Ethics

Financial Statements, Analysis, and Ethics

This objectives of this module include:

(1) An <u>overview of financial accounting</u> and financial statements;
(2) An understanding of <u>basic accounting conventions</u> and how they affect financial statements;
(3) An introduction to the <u>three basic financial statements;</u>
(4) A <u>framework for performing a financial statement analysis</u> to gauge the health and performance of a business;
(5) An application of the <u>Strategic Profit Model</u> as an overall assessment of profit, asset, and financial management; and
(6) An understanding of the <u>ethical issues</u> that have arisen through the manipulation of financial statements

---

Financial Decisions and the Financial Tool Box

The Objective Function
Maximize the Value of the Firm

Basic Corporate Financial Decisions
1) The Investment Decision: Allocating scarce resources across competing uses?
2) The Financing Decision: Raising funds to finance these projects?
3) The Dividend Decision: Rreturning Funds to investors?

The Corporate Financial Toolbox

| Accounting Statements and Ratios | Present Value | Risk and Return Models | Spreadsheet Modelling |

Which is the Biggest Public Accounting Firm?

ARTHUR ANDERSEN

Deloitte & Touche LLP

ᴱᵁ ERNST & YOUNG
FROM THOUGHT TO FINISH.™

KPMG

PRICEWATERHOUSECOOPERS 🔲

Major Internal and External Stakeholder Groups

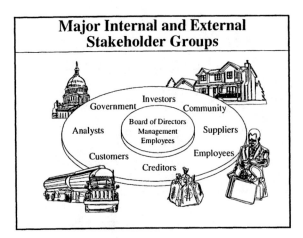

Government
Investors
Community
Analysts
Board of Directors
Management
Employees
Suppliers
Customers
Employees
Creditors

What is GAAP?

GAAP is an acronym that stands for Generally Accepted Accounting Principles. Members of the accounting profession, through associations and individual input into the process, have over the years worked to establish accounting principles accepted by both the accounting profession and the public that relies on the profession's expertise.

Financial Reporting

The **balance sheet** reports, as of a certain point in time, the resources of a company (the assets), the company's obligations (the liabilities), and the equity of the owners.	The **income statement** reports, for a certain interval, the net assets generated through business operations (revenues), the net assets consumed (the expenses), and the net income.	The **statement of cash flows** reports, for a certain interval, the amount of cash generated and consumed by a company through operating, financing, and investing activities.

Financial Reporting

Accounting estimates and judgments are outlined in the **notes to financial statements.**

Basic Accounting Concepts
The Uses of Financial Statements

◆ **Administrative Control**

◆ **Resource Allocation**

◆ **Management Stewardship**

Evolution of Approach to Financial Statements

- After Great Depression: **Focus on Balance Sheet**
- Investors Avoided Stocks Trading Above Book Value
- Cautious With Leverage
- Today: Market Places Value on Both Tangible and Intangibles Assets
- Today, DJIA Trades At 8x Book Value

Basic Accounting Concepts
Financial Statement Terminology

- Sales
  - Revenues

- Cost of Goods Sold
  - Cost of Sales (Revenues)

- Net Earnings
  - Net Profits
  - Net Income

- Shareholders' Equity
  - Net Worth
  - Common Equity
  - Stockholders' Equity

- Fixed Assets
  - Property, Plant and Equipment

Financial Statements
The Balance Sheet Identity

Assets = Liabilities + Equity

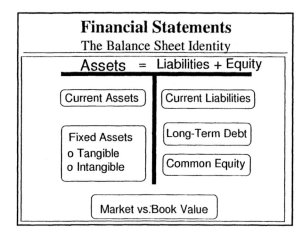

Financial Statements
The Balance Sheet Identity

Assets = Liabilities + Equity

- Current Assets
- Current Liabilities
- Fixed Assets
  - o Tangible
  - o Intangible
- Long-Term Debt
- Common Equity

Market vs. Book Value

Balance Sheet

(in millions of USD)	As of January 31.		
	2003	2004	2005
Assets			
Cash & Cash Equivalents	758	716	2,245
Accounts & Notes Receivable	5,565	5,776	5,069
Inventories	4,760	5,343	5,384
Other Current Assets	852	1,093	1,224
Total Current Assets	11,935	12,928	13,922
Fixed Assets, Net	15,307	16,969	17,066
Other assets	1,361	1,495	1,305
Total Assets	28,603	31,392	32,293
Liabilities			
Accounts Payable	6,548	7,448	7,716
Short-Term Debt	975	866	504
Total Current Liabilities	7,523	8,314	8,220
Long-Term Debt	10,186	10,217	9,034
Other Long-Term Liabilities	1,451	1,796	2,010
Total Liabilities	19,160	20,327	19,264
Stockholders' Equity			
Common Stock	76	76	74
Capital Surplus	1,260	1,344	1,807
Retained Earnings	8,107	9,645	11,148
Total Stockholders' Equity	9,443	11,065	13,029
Total Liabilities + Equity	28,603	31,392	32,293

Notes to Financial Statements

Accounts Receivable

Through our special purpose subsidiary, Target Receivables Corporation (TRC), we transfer, on an ongoing basis, substantially all of our receivables to the Target Credit Card Master Trust (the Trust) in exchange for certificates representing undivided interests in the Trust's assets. TRC owns the undivided interest in the Trust's assets.

Inventory		
millions	2001	2000
Target	$5,248	$5,000
Mervyn's	923	561
Marshall Field's	348	396
Other	330	291
Total Inventory	$4,449	$4,248

Owned and Leased Store Locations

At year-end, owned, leased and "combined" (a combination owned and leased) store locations by operating segment were as follows:

	Owned	Leased	Combined	Total
Target	845	92	126	1,053
Mervyn's	108	91	47	264
Marshall Field's	51	12	1	64
Total	1,042	195	174	1,361

Long-term Debt and Notes Payable				
millions	February 2, 2002		February 3, 2001	
	Rate*	Balance	Rate*	Balance
Notes payable	1.8%	$ 100	5.8%	$ 968
Notes and debentures:				
Due 2001-2005	5.3	3,070	7.4	2,109
Due 2006-2010	6.4	3,660	7.1	1,896
Due 2011-2015	8.9	159	8.9	174
Due 2016-2020	9.7	135	9.7	135
Due 2021-2025	8.3	616	8.3	618
Due 2026-2030	8.7	400	8.7	403
Due 2031-2037	7.0	700		–
Total notes payable, notes and debentures	6.3%	$8,940	7.2%	$6,335
Capital lease obligations		153		156
Less current portion		(905)		(857)
Long-term debt and notes payable		$8,068		$5,634

Basic Accounting Concepts
Income Statement

Fundamental Concepts

- ◆ **GAAP and the Income Statement**

- ◆ **Non-Cash Items**

- ◆ **Time and Costs**

Financial Statements
The Income Statement

- ◆ **GAAP and the Income Statement**
  - Revenue - Expenses = Net Income
  - GAAP - Matching of Costs with Revenues

- ◆ **Non-Cash Items**
  - Especially Depreciation
  - Matching of Costs With Revenues

- ◆ **Time and Costs**
  - Fixed vs. Variable Costs
  - Product Costs - (RM, DL, and OH)
  - Period Costs (SGA)

Basic Accounting Concepts
What Do Earnings Measure?

Fundamental Concepts

- ◆ **Realization Principle Revenue is Recognized When a Good or Service is Provided**

- ◆ **Matching Principle Expenses Incurred in Providing a Good or Service are Recognized in the Period That the Sale is Made**

Income Statement

Sales	xxxx
- Cost of Good Sold	xxx
= Gross Income (Profit)	xxx
-SG&A Expenses	xx
-R&D Expense	xx
-Depreciation	xx
=Operating Income (Profit)	xx
-Interest Expense	xx
=Profit Before Taxes	xx
-Taxes	xx
=Net Income (Profit)	xx

(in millions of USD)	2003	2004	2005
Sales	43,917	48,163	46,839
Cost of Goods Sold	29,260	31,790	31,445
Gross Profit	14,657	16,373	15,394
SG&A	10,181	11,534	10,534
Other Operating Expenses	1,212	1,320	1,259
Earning Before Interest & Taxes	3,264	3,519	3,601
Interest Expense	588	559	570
Earning Before Taxes	2,676	2,960	3,031
Income Tax Expense	1,022	1,119	1,146
Income from Continuing Operations	1,654	1,841	1,885
Gain from Sale of Discontinued Operations	-	-	1,313
Net Income	1,654	1,841	3,198
Earnings Per Share Figures			
Weighted Average Shares- Basic	908.00	911.00	903.80
Weighted Average Shares- Diluted	914.30	919.20	912.10
Basic EPS (Continuing Operations)	1.82	2.02	2.09
Diluted EPS (Continuing Operations)	1.81	2.00	2.07
Stock Price (end of fiscal yr.)	28.21	37.90	50.77

Notes to Financial Statements

Significant Accounting Policies

Revenues   Revenue from retail sales is recognized at the time of sale. Commissions earned on sales generated by leased departments are included within sales. Net credit revenues are comprised of finance charges and late fees on credit sales and third-party merchant fees earned from the use of our Target Visa credit card.

Cost of sales   Cost of sales includes the cost of merchandise sold calculated utilizing the retail inventory accounting method. It includes estimates of shortage that are adjusted upon physical inventory counts in subsequent periods and estimates of amounts due from vendors for certain merchandise allowances and rebates. These estimates are consistent with our historical experience. It also includes a LIFO provision that is calculated based on inventory levels, markup rates and internally generated retail price indices.

Selling, general and administrative expense   Selling, general and administrative expense includes expenses related to store operation, distribution, advertisement and administration. It also includes estimates for the present value cost of workers' compensation and general liability claims.

Statement of Cash Flow

- **Cash Flows From Operating Activities**
  - Net Cash Generated From Selling Product or Service
- **Cash Flows From Investing Activities**
  - Net Cash From Investments In or Disposition of Fixed Assets or Acquisitions
- **Cash Flows From Financing Activities**
  - Cash From Sources of Funding

(in millions of USD)	2003	2004	2005
Operating Activities			
Net Income (from continuing operation)	1,654	1,841	3,198
Depreciation and Amortization	1,212	1,320	1,259
Adjustment to Net Income	934	846	(437)
Changes in A/R	(2,194)	(744)	(209)
Changes in Inventories	(311)	(583)	(853)
Changes in Curr. Liabilities	424	912	1,064
Change in Other Op. Activities	(129)	(432)	(827)
Cash Flow from Operations	1,590	3,160	3,195
Investing Activities			
Capital Expenditures for PPE	(3,221)	(3,004)	(3,068)
Other Investing Activities	32	85	4,247
Cash Flow from Investing	(3,189)	(2,919)	1,179
Financing Activities			
Dividends	(218)	(237)	(272)
Sale (Purchase) of Stock	(14)	0	(1,144)
Net Borrowings	2,082	(72)	(1,477)
Other Financing Activities	8	26	56
Cash Flow from Financing	1,858	(283)	(2,837)
Beginning Cash Balance	499	758	716
Net Change in Cash	259	(42)	1,537
Exchanges Rate Adjustment			(8)
Ending Cash Balance	758	716	2,245

Financial Statement Links

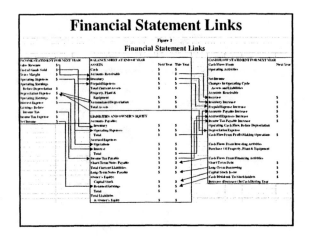

Figure 1
Financial Statement Links

70

Financial Analysis

- Common Size Financial Statements
- Ratio Analysis
- Strategic Profit Model and Assessment of Profit, Asset, and Financial Management

Financial Statements
Common Size Financial Statements

- Common Size Income Statement
  - All Accounts Expressed as a Percent of Net Sales

- Common Size Balance Sheet
  - All Asset Accounts Exressed as a Percent of Total Assets
  - All Liability/Equity Accounts Exressed as a Percent of Total Liabilities + Equity

(in millions of USD)	As of January 31,		
	2003	2004	2005
Assets			
Cash & Cash Equivalents	2.7%	2.3%	7.0%
Accounts & Notes Receivable	19.5%	18.4%	15.7%
Inventories	16.6%	17.0%	16.7%
Other Current Assets	3.0%	3.5%	3.8%
Total Current Assets	41.7%	41.2%	43.1%
Fixed Assets, Net	53.5%	54.1%	52.8%
Other assets	4.8%	4.8%	4.0%
Total Assets	100.0%	100.0%	100.0%
Liabilities			
Accounts Payable	22.9%	23.7%	23.9%
Short-Term Debt	3.4%	2.8%	1.6%
Total Current Liabilities	26.3%	26.5%	25.5%
Long-Term Debt	35.6%	32.5%	28.0%
Other Long-Term Liabilities	5.1%	5.7%	6.2%
Total Liabilities	67.0%	64.8%	59.7%
Stockholders' Equity			
Common Stock	0.3%	0.2%	0.2%
Capital Surplus	4.4%	4.3%	5.6%
Retained Earnings	28.3%	30.7%	34.5%
Total Stockholders' Equity	33.0%	35.2%	40.3%
Total Liabilities + Equity	100.0%	100.0%	100.0%

71

(in millions of USD)	2003	2004	2005
Sales	100.0%	100.0%	100.0%
Cost of Goods Sold	66.6%	66.0%	67.1%
Gross Profit	33.4%	34.0%	32.9%
SG&A	23.2%	23.9%	22.5%
Other Operating Expenses	2.8%	2.7%	2.7%
Earning Before Interest & Taxes	7.4%	7.3%	7.7%
Interest Expense	1.3%	1.2%	1.2%
Earning Before Taxes	6.1%	6.1%	6.5%
Income Tax Expense	2.3%	2.3%	2.4%
Income from Continuing Operations	3.8%	3.8%	4.0%
Gain from Sale of Discontinued Operations	0.0%	0.0%	2.8%
Net Income	3.8%	3.8%	6.8%

Basic Financial Analysis

- **Liquidity Ratios**
- **Activity Measures**
- **Leverage Ratios**
- **Profitability Measures**
- **Valuation Ratios**

Financial Statements

Liquidity Ratios

- Measures Firm's Ability to Meet Short-Term Obligations
- Closely Related to Size and Composition of Working Capital Position
- Other Things Equal, Higher Working Capital Implies More Liquid Position

Current Ratio

- Indicates Amount of Current Assets Available to Meet Maturing Obligations Listed Under Current Liabilities
- Creditors Look At Ratio to Judge "Cushion" Between Current Obligations and Firm's Liquid Assets

Quick Ratio

- Also Known As Acid-Test Ratio
- More Conservative Measure of Liquidity
- Takes Inventory Off Before Measuring Liquidity
- Inventory Cannot Be Used to Readily Settle Claims

Financial Statement Analysis
Liquidity Ratios

Activity Ratios

- Asset Utilization Ratios
- Measures How Well Firm Uses Productive Resources
- Related to Amount of Sales Generated Per Dollar Invested In Particular Asset
- Related to Receivables, Inventory, Total Assets

Inventory Turnover

- Index of How Fast Goods Flow Through Inventory
- For Retail Companies: From Purchase to Sale
- For Manufacturing Company: From Raw Material to Sale
- Computed By Dividing Cost of Goods Sold (COGS) By Inventory

Receivables Turnover

- Measures Number of Times Receivables Turn Over During the Year
- Higher It Is, Shorter the Time Between Sales and Collection
- Indicates How Well Firm Manages Credit and Collection Policies

_____
_____
_____
_____
_____
_____
_____

Financial Statement Analysis
Activity Ratios

_____
_____
_____
_____
_____
_____
_____

Payables Turnover

- Measures Number of Times Payables Turn Over During the Year
- Lower It Is, Longer the Time Company Takes to Pay Its Creditors
- Indicates How Well Firm Manages Its Payables

_____
_____
_____
_____
_____
_____
_____

Financial Statement Analysis
Activity Ratios

Financial Leverage Ratios

■ Measure Risk Focusing On Financing Mix

■ Examine Extent to Which Firm Uses Debt to Finance Operations

■ Examine Balance Sheet: Higher Leverage Result In Higher Risk

■ Examine Income Statement: Coverage Ratios

Times Interest Earned

■ Measures Firm's Ability to Handle Debt

■ More Important Than Level of Debt Itself

■ Ratio Indicates Number of Times Firm's Operating Earnings (EBIT) Can "Cover" Its Interest Expense

Financial Statement Analysis
Financial Leverage Ratios

Profitability Ratios

- Also Known As Operating Ratios
- Vital In Assessing Managers' Performance
- Examples:
- Profit Margin
- Return on Assets
- Return on Equity

Profit Margin

- Measures Firm's Ability to Control Its Expenses In Relation to Sales
- Declining Margin Normally an Indication of Increasing Expense and/or Decreasing Sales
- Useful to Investors For Measuring Manager's Performance

ROA and ROE

- ROA – Return on Assets
- Focuses on Earning Power of Going Operations and Assets
- ROE – Return on Equity
- Measures Return on Stockholders' Equity
- Increase In ROA and ROE Often Result In Stock Price Appreciation

---

Financial Statement Analysis
Profitability Ratios

Valuation Ratios

- Determine Value Investors Place On Company
- Examples:
- Price/Earnings Ratio (P/E)
- Market-to-Book Ratio
- Market Capitalization

Financial Statement Analysis
Market Valuation Ratios

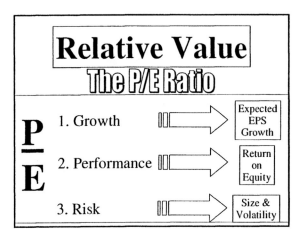

Relative Value
The P/E Ratio

$\dfrac{P}{E}$

1. Growth ⟹ Expected EPS Growth

2. Performance ⟹ Return on Equity

3. Risk ⟹ Size & Volatility

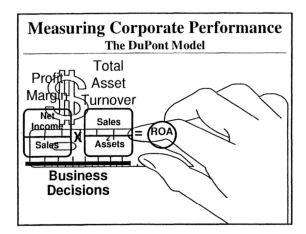

Measuring Corporate Performance
The DuPont Model

Profit Margin — Total Asset Turnover

$\dfrac{\text{Net Income}}{\text{Sales}} \times \dfrac{\text{Sales}}{\text{Assets}} = \text{ROA}$

Business Decisions

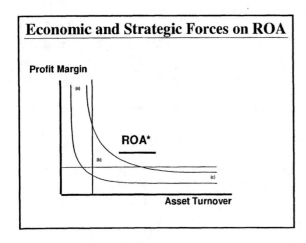

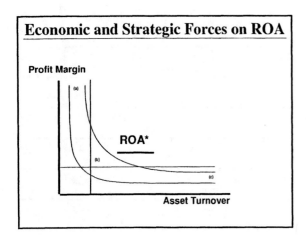

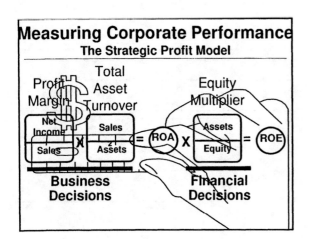

Measuring Corporate Performance
The Strategic Profit Model
ROS * Turnover = ROA * Leverage = ROE

Financial Ethics

Reading the Headlines

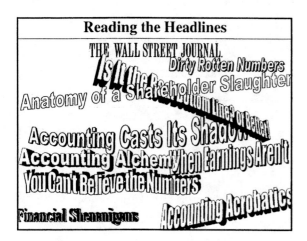

THE WALL STREET JOURNAL

Dirty Rotten Numbers

Is It the Shareholder Slaughter

Anatomy of a

Accounting Casts Its Shadow

Accounting Alchemy When Earnings Aren't

You Can't Believe the Numbers

Financial Shenanigans

Accounting Acrobatics

THE WALL STREET JOURNAL

Computer Associates' Revenue Is Probed by Federal Officials

By JERRY GUIDERA
Staff Reporter of THE WALL STREET JOURNAL

Federal authorities are trying to determine whether Computer Associates International Inc. wrongly booked over $ revenue in its 1998 and 1999 fiscal years as part of a scheme the company's senior managers

Revenue Doping?

By JESSE EISINGER
Staff Reporter of THE WALL STREET JOURNAL

As if pharmaceuticals investors didn't have enough to worry about, now come concerns about channel stuffing — meaning that pharmacies might have stocked up on more drugs than they are selling to patients

Investors should look the wake of Pfizer's money owed by custo despite a decline in sa sold more than the us

SEC Broadens Accounting Inquiries, Opening a Record Number of Cases

By SUSAN PULLIAM
Staff Reporter of THE WALL STREET JOURNAL

The Securities and Exchange Commission is looking into accounting methods at some of the nation's largest companies, broadening the scope of its inquiry beyond the accounting issues raised by the collapse of Enron Corp. to include a laundry list of other potential accounting abuses

Adelphia's Related-Party Deals Become Focus in Federal Probe

By DEBORAH SOLOMON, ROBERT FRANK and JERRY MARKON
Staff Reporters of THE WALL STREET JOURNAL

Federal prosecutors conducting criminal investigations into Adelphia Communications Corp. are focusing on a number of questionable related-party transactions and possible accounting irregularities involving the company's founding Rigas family, according to people familiar with the probes

SEC Broadens Its Investigation Into Revenue-Boosting Tricks

By SUSAN PULLIAM
Staff Reporter of THE

REVVED UP

Securities and Exchange explanation of tran business across

about an boosting ping

nergy Inc., any engaged in Questions trading from misleading market during the

Financial Ethics: GAAP vs. GAP

Generally Accepted Accounting Principles
Issued by FASB; Ultimate Regulation is by the SEC

GAP

The Financial Numbers Game

■**Aggressive accounting** - A forceful and intentional choice and <u>application of accounting principles done in an effort to achieve desired results</u>, typically higher current earnings, whether the practices followed are in accordance with GAAP or not

■**Earnings management** - The active manipulation of <u>earnings toward a predetermined target</u>, which may be set by management, a forecast made by analysts, or an amount that is consistent with a smoother, more sustainable earnings stream

■**Income smoothing** - A form of earnings management designed <u>to remove peaks and valleys</u> from a normal earnings series, including steps to reduce and "store" profits during good years for use during slower years

■**Fraudulent financial reporting** - <u>Intentional misstatements or omissions</u> of amounts or disclosures in financial statements, done to deceive financial statement users, that are determined to be fraudulent by an administrative, civil, or criminal proceeding

■**Creative accounting practices** - <u>Any and all steps used to play the financial numbers game</u>, including the aggressive choice and application of accounting principles fraudulent financial reporting, and any steps taken toward earnings management or income smoothing

Source: Charles Mulford and Eugene Comiskey, *The Financial Numbers Game* (John Wiley & Sons, 2002).

Primary Accounting Issues

1. Aggressive - Fraudulent Revenue Recognition
2. Aggressive - Fraudulent Capitalization of Expenses
3. Failure to Record Liabilities

83

Cooking the Books

Schilit's Seven Financial Shenanigans

1. **Recording revenue too soon**
2. **Recording bogus revenue**
3. **Boosting income with one-time gains**
4. **Shifting current expenses to a later or earlier period**
5. **Failing to disclose all liabilities**
6. **Shifting current income to a later period**
7. **Shifting future expenses into the current period**

Source: Howard Schilit, *Financial Shenanigans* (McGraw Hill, 2002).

No. 1 - Recording Revenue Too Soon

Revenue Should be Recognized Once an Exchange has Occurred

No. 1 - Recording Revenue Too Soon

Shipping goods before sale is finalized

1. Billing in advance
2. Shipping defective goods
3. Using an aggressive revenue approach

No. 1 - Recording Revenue Too Soon

Recording revenue when important uncertainties exist

1. Is the sale with or without recourse?
2. Does the buyer have financing to pay?
3. Is there an obligation by the buyer to pay?

Recording revenue before shipment or customer's unconditional acceptance

Recording revenue although customer is not obligated to pay

Selling to an affiliated party

Giving customer something of value as a quid pro quo

No. 1 - Recording Revenue Too Soon

Recording revenue when future services are still due

1. Booking future revenue

Enron

Booked PV of differences between 5 year sales contract to utility & 5 year purchase contract from supplier at time of inception.

No. 2 - Recording Bogus Revenue

Revenue Should be Recognized Once an Exchange has Occurred

No. 2 - Recording Bogus Revenue

Management records refunds from suppliers as revenue

Recording sales lacking economic substance – side agreements

Recording cash received from lender as revenue

Recording investment income as revenue

Recording as revenue supplier rebates tied to future required purchases

Release revenue improperly "held back" before a merger

Inventory games

Reliant Resources.

Recorded Bogus Revenue

Revenue for the years 1999-2001 was overstated by $7.8 billion due to the recording of "round-trip" energy trades. These types of energy trades involved Reliant Energy buying and then selling an equal amount of a commodity in order to artificially inflate revenues.

No. 3 - Boosting Income with One-Time Gains

Revenue Should be Recognized Once an Exchange has Occurred and Similarly, Report Gains only after an Exchange has taken Place

No. 3 - Boosting Income with One-Time Gains

We bring good things to life.

- Management sells undervalued asset
- Recording gains selling assets recorded at deflated book value
- Including investment income or gains as revenue
- Including investment income as reduction in operating expenses
- Creating income by reclassification of investment gains s

No. 4 – Shift Expenses to a Later Period

Capitalize Costs that Produce a Future Benefit and Expense Those that Produce no Such Benefit

---

No. 4 – Shift Expenses to a Later Period

Management improperly capitalizes costs

1. Start-up costs
2. R&D costs
3. Advertising expenditures
4. Administrative costs

No. 4 – Shift Expenses to a Later Period

Management depreciates or amortizes costs too slowly

1. Excessively long amortization periods
2. Increases in depreciation /amortization schedules

Key Issues:
What is normal industry practice?
Is the industry experiencing rapid technological change?

No. 4 – Shift Expenses to a Later Period

Management fails to write-off worthless assets

Changing accounting policies and shift current expenses to an earlier period

Amortizing costs too slowly

Releasing asset reserves into income

Waste Management
A Case Study in Value Destruction

WASTE MANAGEMENT

Washington, D.C., March 26, 2002 — The Securities and Exchange Commission filed suit today against the founder and five other former top officers of Waste Management Inc., charging them with perpetrating a massive financial fraud lasting more than five years. The complaint, filed in U.S. District Court in Chicago, charges that defendants engaged in a systematic scheme to falsify and misrepresent Waste Management's financial results between 1992 and 1997.

"Our complaint describes one of the most egregious accounting frauds we have seen," said Thomas C. Newkirk, associate director of the SEC's Division of Enforcement. "For years, these defendants cooked the books, enriched themselves, preserved their jobs, and duped unsuspecting shareholders."

Waste Management
A Case Study in Value Destruction

WASTE MANAGEMENT

Accounting Issues
Avoiding depreciation expenses on garbage trucks
Assigning arbitrary salvage values to assets that previously had no salvage value
Failing to record expenses of landfills as they were filled with waste
Refusing to record expenses of unsuccessful and abandoned landfill projects
Established inflated environmental reserves
Improperly capitalized expenses
Failed to establish sufficient reserves to pay for income taxes and other expenses

Source: U.S. Securities and Exchange Commission, 26 March 2002: 2002: 44

Waste Management
A Case Study in Value Destruction

WASTE MANAGEMENT

Overstated Profits:

$1.7B

Shareholder Value Loss:

$6.0B

The Downside of Accounting Manipulation

Waste Management Inc.

Copyright 2000 Yahoo! Inc.   http://finance.yahoo.com/

WORLDCOM

CREATIVE ACCOUNTING

By booking certain costs as a capital expense, WorldCom was able to boost its bottom line. A look at how the company conducted such accounting in 2001.

WorldCom's accounting

❶ Accounts $3.1 billion in 'line costs,' including telecom access and transport charges, as capital expenditure.

❷ Plans to amortize $5.1 billion over a period of time, possibly as much as 10 years.

❸ Reports net income of $1.38 billion for 2001.

Generally accepted accounting principles

Ⓐ The $3.1 billion 'line-cost' expense is booked as an operating expense.

Ⓑ The entire $3.1 billion would have been counted as a cost of business for that quarter.

Ⓒ Net income for 2001 would have been a loss, amount to be determined.

No. 5 – Fail to Record / Disclose all Liabilities

A Firm incurs a Liability if it has an Obligation to make Future Sacrifices

No. 5 – Fail to Record / Disclose all Liabilities

Failing to record expenses (and related liabilities) when future obligations remain

Reducing liabilities by changing accounting assumptions

Releasing questionable liability reserves into income

Creating sham rebates

Recording revenue when cash is received, yet future obligations remain

No. 5 – Fail to Record / Disclose all Liabilities

Management fails to accrue expected or contingent liabilities

Accrue loss when:
» There is a probable loss
» The amount is reasonably estimated

No. 5 – Fail to Record / Disclose all Liabilities

Management engages in transactions to keep debt off the books

FASB attempting to correct:
- » Swaps
- » In-substance defeasance of debt
- » Defined-benefit pensions
- » Operating leases
- » Subs & joint ventures
- » Special purpose entities

No. 6 – Shift Current Income to a Later Period

Record Revenue/Expenses in the Period in Which it is Earned

No. 6 – Shift Current Income to a Later Period

Management creates reserves to shift income to a later period

Cookie-Jar Reserves
Smooth income through the use of reserves

Improperly holding back revenue just before an acquisition closes

No. 7 – Shift Future Expenses to the Current Period

Charge Expenses Against Income in the Period in Which the Benefit is Received

---

No. 7 – Shift Future Expenses to the Current Period

Management accelerates discretionary expenses into the current period

Prepayment of operating expenses

Shorter "life" means higher expense each period

Improperly write off in-process R&D costs from acquisition

No. 7 – Shift Future Expenses to the Current Period

Management has the firm "take the big bath"

New management often writes-off old projects to relieve future periods of the expenses

Large nonrecurring gains offset with large expenses, or vice versa

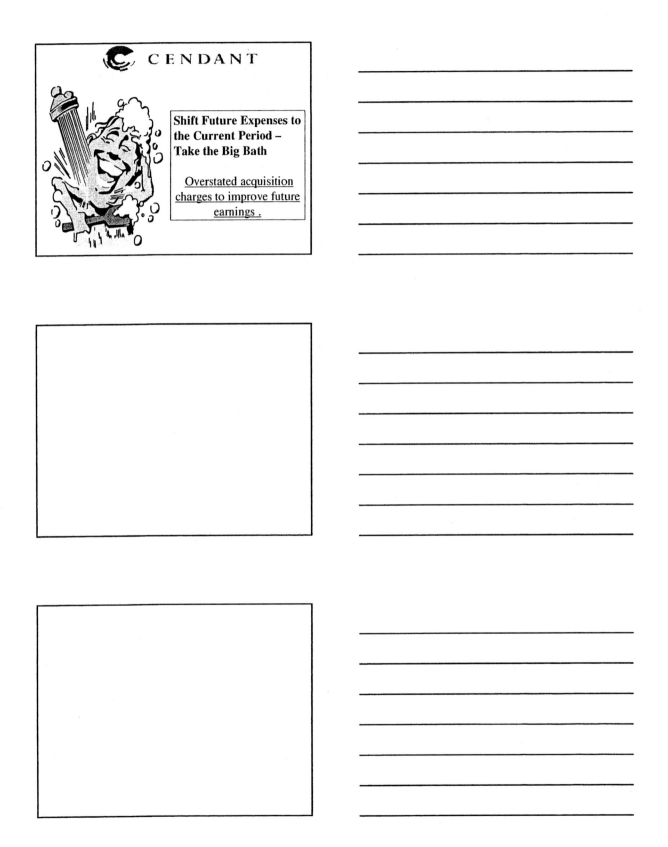

CENDANT

**Shift Future Expenses to the Current Period –
Take the Big Bath**

Overstated acquisition
charges to improve future
earnings .

The Financial
Life Cycle

The Financial Life Cycle

This module examines the financial life cycle of a firm.
It covers the capital raising process, the primary securities
market, and mergers and acquisitions. Objectives for
this module include:

(1) Understanding the role of the SEC as the regulator
of the primary securities markets;
(2) Review the financing life cycle and sources of
capital of a firm;
(3) Explore the primary securities market and the
securities issuance process;
(4) Identify current themes and trends in the primary
securities market
(5) Provide an introduction to mergers and acquisitions.

The SEC as Regulator

Primary Roles/Goals

1. Protect Investors

2. Information Disclosure

3. Operational and
Pricing Efficiency of
Security Markets

4. Fair and Orderly
Markets

The SEC as Regulator

Procedural Elements of the SEC

1. Rules and Regulations

2. Enforcement Action

3. Provide for Full and Fair Disclosure of Information - Quarterly and Annual Filing Requirements

---

PROPRIETARY INFORMATION

Nvidia Corporation Is The Worldwide Leader Of Graphics Processors and Media Communications Devices

Designs, Develops and Markets 3D Graphics Processors, Graphics Processing Units, And Related Software For Every Type Of Desktop Personal Computer

Increases in Revenue and Net Income Reflect Strong Demand For New Products At Higher Average Selling Prices

Financial Data

Market Cap $6.981 billion

Revenue: 1999- $158M, 2000- $374.5M, 2001- $735M

Contract Info

Contract Involving Manufacture Of Graphics Chip For Microsoft's Xbox

Share Price More Than Doubled After Contract Announcement On March 10, 2000

Production of Chips Began In May, Could Bring in Revenue Of $2 billion

Case Info

Charges Brought Against 15 People In November 2001

Case Involves All Lower-Level Employees And Their Friends/Relatives

Insiders Alleged To Have Earned $1.7

2 Defendants Have Settled Charges By Returning Gains, Without Admitting Wrongdoing

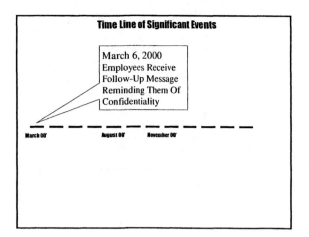

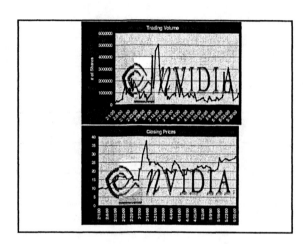

Elliott Spitzer as Market Regulator

Elliot Spitzer
Attorney General
New York

Wall Street Analysts
$1.5B Settlement With
Major Brokerage Firms
For Tainted Research

Mutual Funds
Settlements With Major
Investment Companies who
Allowed Favored Customers
To Execute 'Market Timing'
Trades

The Financing Life Cycle

Mergers &
Acquisitions

Security
Offerings

Venture
Capital/
Private
Equity

Bank
Financing

Owner's
Capital

The Financing Life Cycle

Owners Capital
Initial Capital Investment
of Owners

Bank Financing
Loans and Lines-of-Credit
From Financial Institutions

Venture Capital
Equity Investments
by Investors in
Private Companies

Venture Capital Financing

Risk Capital
Debt/Equity Capital Required for Growth Once Bank Financing is Unavailable

Required Returns
20 - 50 Percent Expected Return Depending on Stage
VC Exit Strategy (Sell/IPO)

Types of Financing
Depends on Financing Stage

How Venture Capital Works

HOW THE VENTURE CAPITAL INDUSTRY WORKS

The venture capital industry has four main players: entrepreneurs who need funding; investors who want high returns; investment bankers who need companies to sell; and the venture capitalists who make money for themselves by making a market for the other three.

Entrepreneurs — $ — Venture Capitalists — $ — Investment Bankers

Ideas — IPOs — STOCK

Corporations And Government — Private Investors — Public Markets And Corporations

Venture Capital Financing

Seed/Startup Funding
Earliest stage of business, typically no operating history. Investment is based on a business plan, the management group backgrounds along with the market and financial projections.

First Round Funding
Typically funding that accomodates growth. Company may have finished R&D. Funding is often in the form of convertible bond.

Intermediate/Second Round Funding
Maturing company where a future leveraged buyout, merger or acquisition and/or initial public offering is a viable option.

Later Stage Funding
Mature company where funds are needed to support major expansion or new product development. Company is profitable or breakeven.

Venture Capital Financing

Later Stage Funding
Mature company where funds are needed to support major expansion or new product development. Company is profitable or breakeven.

Equity Loan
Offer of an ownership position to induce the loan or can be a note that has an option to convert from debt to equity.

Mezzanine Funding
Company's progress makes positioning for an Initial Public Offering viable. Venture funds are used to support the IPO.

The Lifecycle of a Venture Capital Deal
CacheFlow

- **March 13, 1996** - CacheFlow Founded by Michael Malcolm with $1M from 'Angels'. Design and Produce a Caching Appliance for Faster Internet Pages

- **October 1996** - Benchmark Capital Buys 25% of CacheFlow (3.2M 'A' Shares @ $.875). Remaining 75% Owned by Management and Angels

- **Jan-Nov 1997** - Development and Testing of Product - Ready

- **December 1997** - Still with no Revenues, US Venture Partners Pays $6 M ('B' Shares @ $2.28) for 17% of Firm. Benchmark Chips in $1.8M to Retain 25%

- **May 1998** - Revenues of $800,000 for Year

The Lifecycle of a Venture Capital Deal
CacheFlow

- **June 1998** - Investment Bankers Come Calling

- **March 1999** - Tech Exec Brian NeSmith Hired as CEO.
  New VC Financing - 'C' Shares @ $4.575/Share
  Technology X-Over Ventures - $8.7M for 7%
  Benchmark - $3.4M to Retain 18%
  US Venture Partners - $2.1M to Retain 12%

- **August 1999** - MSDW and CSFB Hired as Investment Banker

- **September 1999** - S-1 Filed - 5M Shares or 15.6% of Company Revenues - $3.8 M - Net Loss - (13.2M)

- **November 1999** - IPO @ $24 on Nov 19

The Lifecycle of a Venture Capital Deal

CacheFlow

◆ November 19, 1999   - CacheFlow Stock Closes @ $126/Share on First Day of Trading

            <u>Stock Performance</u>
            'A' Shares - $.875 - $126 - 14,342%
            'B' Shares - $2.28 - $126 - 5,491%
            'C' Shares - $4.575 - $126 - 2,662%

◆ April 2000   - <u>Stock @ $112 - VC Investment Performance</u>
            Benchmark - $8.0M to $537M
            US Venture Partners - $8.1M to $351M
            Technology X-Over Ventures - $8.7M to $213M
            Mr. Malcolm - 5.1M Shares - $576M

CacheFlow Stock Performance

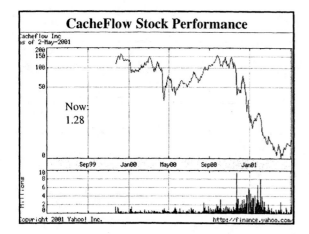

CacheFlow becomes Blue Coat

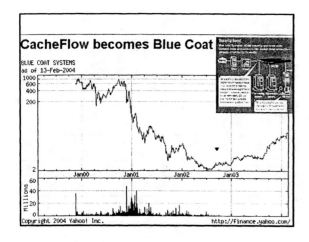

100

Venture Capital Investment Criteria

People, People, People

Market Opportunities

Partners
Early Investors
Corporations

Sector Growth

Financials

BOWMAN
CAPITAL MANAGEMENT. LLC

Securities Markets

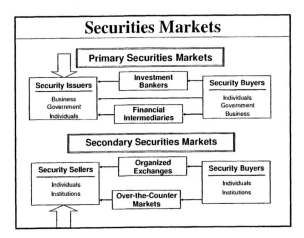

The Role of Securities Markets

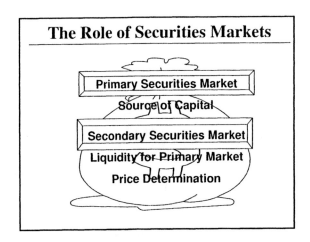

The Financing Life Cycle

Initial Public Offering (IPO)
Initial Public Sale of Common Stock to Investors

Seasoned Offerings
Subsequent Sales of Common Stock to Investors

Also Known as Secondary Offerings

ANATOMY OF A DEAL

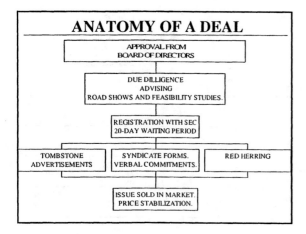

The Primary Securities Markets

Investment Banking and Security Issuances

1. Advising

2. Origination (Securities Act of 1933)
   – Due Diligence, Registration Statement, Prospectus

3. Syndicate Formation, Underwriting, and Price Stabilization

Underwriting Syndicate

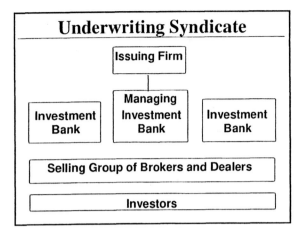

The Primary Securities Market
Security Issuances

◆ **IPOs Versus Secondary Offerings**
- IPO - Initial Sale of Common Stock to Investors in Market
- Secondary Offering - Sales of Common Stock by Publicly-Held Firms

◆ **Registration Statement**
- Filed with the SEC Prior to Selling Securities to Investors

◆ **Prospectus**
Selling Document for Securities

The Primary Securities Market
Security Issuances

◆ **Red Herring**
Preliminary Prospectus

◆ **"Tombstones"**
Issue Advertisement

◆ **Green Shoe**
Underwriter Option to Sell 15% More Shares

◆ **Negotiated Offerings**
- **Underwritings**
- **Best Efforts and Stand-by Offerings**

Public Offering of Securities

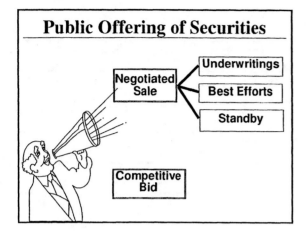

Negotiated Sale
- Underwritings
- Best Efforts
- Standby

Competitive Bid

The Primary Securities Market
The Costs of Security Issuances

→ **Underwriting Spread**
The Difference Between the Price the Issuer Receives and the Offer Price

→ **Other Direct Expenses**
Printing and Legal Expenses

→ **Indirect Expenses**
Company Costs Associated with a Security Issue

Initial Public Offerings

Why Go Public? (IPO)
Capital to Execute Business Plan
Liquidity for Owners
Stock for Compensation and
 Acquisitions
Marketing and Branding
 Opportunity
Capital Market Access

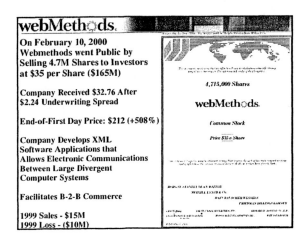

webMethods.

On February 10, 2000 Webmethods went Public by Selling 4.7M Shares to Investors at $35 per Share ($165M)

Company Received $32.76 After $2.24 Underwriting Spread

End-of-First Day Price: $212 (+508%)

Company Develops XML Software Applications that Allows Electronic Communications Between Large Divergent Computer Systems

Facilitates B-2-B Commerce

1999 Sales - $15M
1999 Loss - ($10M)

4,715,000 Shares

webMethods.

Common Stock

Price $35 a Share

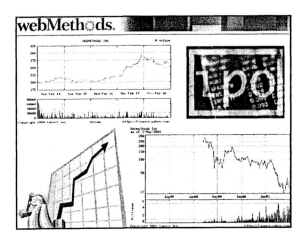

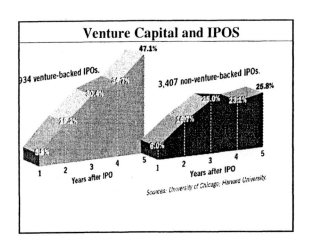

Venture Capital and IPOS

934 venture-backed IPOs.

47.1%

3,407 non-venture-backed IPOs.

25.8%

Years after IPO

Sources: University of Chicago; Harvard University.

Netscape's Initial Public Offering

Netscape went public in August of 1995 at $28 (14) Per Share

The Shares Closed on the First Day of Trading at $58 (29)

Within 6 Months, Netscape was Trading at $180 (90 Per Share)

The Shares Began Falling as soon as Microsoft Focussed its Efforts on the Internet

On November 18, 1998, Netscape Agreed to be Purchased by AOL in a Stock Swap Worth $4.2B

N

NETSCAPE

Netscape's Stock Price History

Netscape Communications Corp
as of 24-Dec-1998   Splits: ▼ S&P ■

(C) 1998 Yahoo! Inc.   Volume (1000's)   http://quote.yahoo.com/

The IPO Hall of Fame

VA Linux Systems	+733%
Theglobe.com	+606%
Foundry Networks	+525%
Webmethods	+508%
FreeMarkets	+483%
Cobalt Networks	+482%
Akamai Tech	+458%
CacheFlow	+427%
Sycamore Networks	+386%
Ask Jeevesom	+364%
Finisar	+357%
Crossroads Systems	+337%
Priceline.com	+331%
Wireless Facilities	+313%
Calico Commerce	+300%

Long Shots

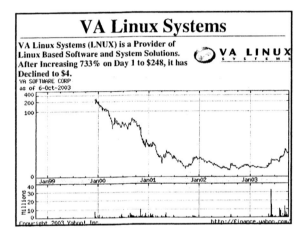

	VA LINUX SYSTEMS	
1999 Sales	$47.1	$18.6
1999 EPS	-1.68	-2.06
1999 ROE	-63.5%	-50.8%
Expected EPS Growth	NMF	NMF
Stock Price	$65	$6
Market Capitalization	$2.7B	$171M
Price/Earnings Ratio	NMF	NMF

Start-Up Businesses that have Attracted Much Investor Interest
Despite Not Demonstrating a Viable and Profitable Business Model

VA Linux Systems

VA Linux Systems (LNUX) is a Provider of
Linux Based Software and System Solutions.
After Increasing 733% on Day 1 to $248, it has
Declined to $4.

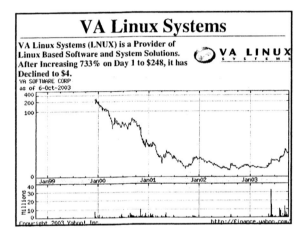

Theglobe.Com

Theglobe.com (TGLO) an Internet Community
IPO ($9 to $63 on Day 1 Followed by 2/1 Split
All-Time High - $80 -- Today - $1 1/2

The Primary Securities Market
Initial Public Offerings (IPOs)

➔ The Initial Sale of Common Stock to the Public by a Company

➔ The Average First Day Return (15%) is Evidence of Underpricing

➔ The Winner's Curse - The Average Investor Does Not Get the First Day Return

➔ The Long-Term (3-Year) Adjusted Performance of IPOs is Negative

The Primary Securities Market
Initial Public Offerings (IPOs)
IPO Adjusted Stock Returns

IPO Stock Return Adjusted for Market and Firm Size, All IPOs 1965-199

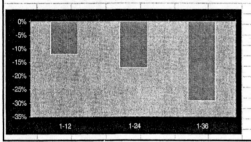

The Primary Securities Market
Seasoned/Secondary Offerings

➔ The Sale of New Common Stock by a Public Company

➔ Using Equity Markets as a Source of Capital to Meet Financing Needs

➔ The Average Return at the Announcement is -3.0%

➔ Seasoned Issues Are a Negative Signal to Investors

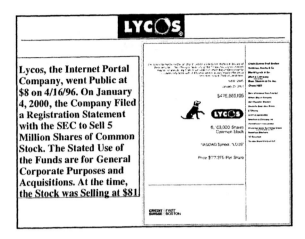

Lycos, the Internet Portal Company, went Public at $8 on 4/16/96. On January 4, 2000, the Company Filed a Registration Statement with the SEC to Sell 5 Million Shares of Common Stock. The Stated Use of the Funds are for General Corporate Purposes and Acquisitions. At the time, the Stock was Selling at $81

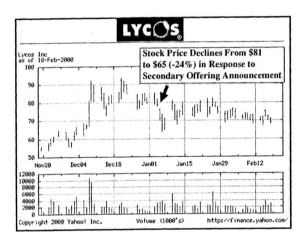

Stock Price Declines From $81 to $65 (-24%) in Response to Secondary Offering Announcement

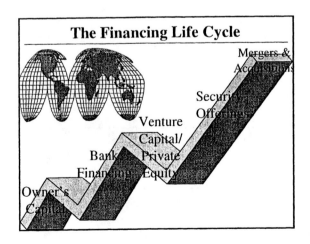

The Financing Life Cycle

Mergers & Acquisitions

Mergers & Acquisitions

Acquisition

| Friendly/Hostile

Merger or
Acquisition

Stock Swap

Cash/Asset Acquisition

Proxy Contest
Board Control

Going Private

Leverage
Buy-Out

U. S. Merger and Acquisition Activity
1980-2002

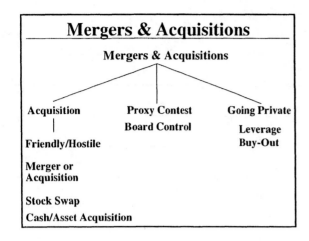

AOL – Time Warner

(January 10, 2000) AOL and Time Warner Announced that
the Two Companies would Merge in a Stock Swap Worth
Nearly $190B. This Represents the Largest Merger in
Market History, and Lifted Internet and Media Stocks
Around the World in Anticipation of Future Consolidation.

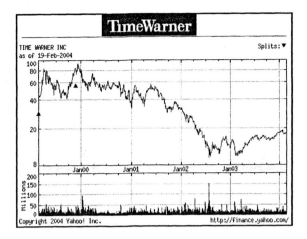

TimeWarner

TIME WARNER INC
as of 19-Feb-2004   Splits: ▼

Copyright 2004 Yahoo! Inc.   http://finance.yahoo.com/

Corporate Takeovers:
The 1980s Versus the 1990s

1980s	1990s
→ Financial Deals	→ Strategic, Convergence, Global
→ Deals were Hostile	→ Deals are Friendly
→ Debt Financed	→ Stock Financed
→ Availability of Financing Led to 1990s Merger Wave	→ Industry Restructuring has Added to 1990s Merger Wave
→ Bad Press	→ Good Press

Business Week

The Merger Hangover

The Value Creation Challenge of Acquisitions

Company Stock Price → **Reflects Discounted Value of Business**

Sources of Synergy Value

- Cost Savings
  - E.g. Economies of Scale
- Revenue Enhancements
  - E.g. Complementary Products
- Process Improvements
  - E.g. Transfer of Best Practices
- Financial Engineering
  - E.g. Reduced Cost of Capital

Why Do Mergers Fail?

- Overpay by Offering a Large Premium, Which Hands the Bulk of Future Gains from the Merger to Shareholders of the Target Company
- Overestimate Cost Savings From Operating Synergies and Revenue Gains from Marketing Synergies
- Slow to Integrate Operations After Merger, Frustrating Customers and Employees
- Obsessed with Cost-Cutting and Not Dealing with Resolving Culture Conflicts

Equity Carve-Outs and Spinoffs

> ### Reverse Merger
> **Break a Company Up by:**
> **1. Equity Carve Out – IPO**
> **In a Subsidiary**
> **2. Spin-Off a Subsidiary**
> **By Distributing Shares in**
> **The Form of a Dividend**

AT&T - Lucent-NCR

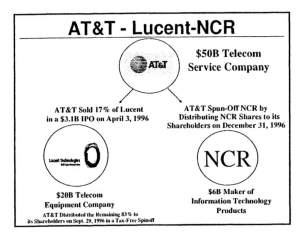

$50B Telecom Service Company

AT&T Sold 17% of Lucent in a $3.1B IPO on April 3, 1996

AT&T Spun-Off NCR by Distributing NCR Shares to its Shareholders on December 31, 1996

$20B Telecom Equipment Company

AT&T Distributed the Remaining 83% to its Shareholders on Sept. 29, 1996 in a Tax-Free Spinoff

$6B Maker of Information Technology Products

Equity Carve Outs

◆ **An Initial Public Offering (IPO) for Some Portion of a Wholly-Owned Subsidiary**

◆ **Generally the Parent Retains at Least 80% Ownership to Qualify for Tax Consolidation and Future Tax-Free Spinoff**

◆ **Either the Parent or the Subsidiary Can Offer the Shares**

◆ **Requires S-1 Registration**

Equity Carve Outs

AT&T - Lucent Technologies

Hewlett Packard – Agilent Technologies

3 Com - Palm

DuPont - Conoco

Sears - Allstate Insurance

The Limited - Intimate Brands

Thermal Electron - 22 ECOs

Spinoffs

◆ A Stock Dividend in the Form of the Stock of a Subsidiary

◆ Usually Structured to Meet IRC Section 355 Requirements as a Tax-Free Spinoff
  - Active Business
  - Business Purpose
  - At Lease 80% Spunoff

◆ Parent Stock Rises 2% at the Announcement On Average

◆ Requires Form 10 SEC Filing

Notable Spinoffs

Sprint - 360 Communications

ITT – ITT Industries – ITT Hartford

GM - EDS

Quaker Oats – Fisher–Price Toys

Pepsico - Tricon

General Mills - Darden Restaurants

Coors – ACX Technologies

Baxter International – Caremark

Pacific Telesis – Air Touch

Host Marriott – Marriott Intl.

American Express - Lehman Bros

Value Creation Through Spinoffs

Company Characteristics	Tight Controls	Entreprenueral
Culture	Tight Controls	Entreprenueral
Capital Intensity	Low	High
Risk	Low	High

_____

_____

_____

_____

_____

_____

_____

_____

_____

_____

_____

_____

_____

_____

_____

_____

_____

_____

Overview of the Financial Markets

Overview of the Financial Markets

This module explores the role and the elements of the financial markets. Objectives for this module include:

(1) Understanding the <u>basic structure</u> of the financial markets;
(2) Exploring the differences between the <u>organized exchanges and the over-the-counter</u> (OTC) market;
(3) Identifying <u>measures of the stock market</u> as well as current issues in the markets

The Role of Financial Markets

- Mobilize Savings and Allocate Funds to Users On Basis of Expected Risk-Adjusted Returns

- Facilitate Risk Transfer

- Provide Liquidity

- Crucial Role In Valuing Financial Assets

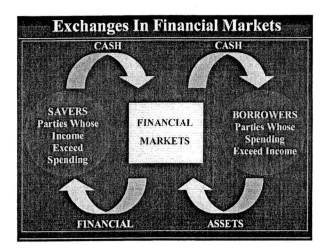

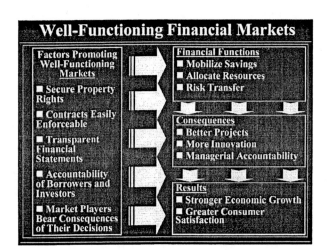

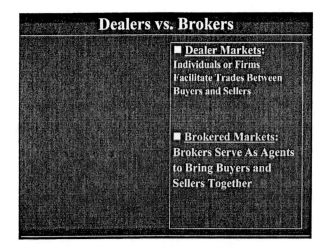

Financial Markets

- **Organized Exchange:** Actual Physical Place For Trading Securities

- **E.g., NYSE and American Stock Exchange**

- **Over-the-Counter Markets:** No Physical Location

- **Dealers Linked By Computer Network**

- **E.g., NASDAQ**

Financial Markets
Organized Exchanges

NYSE   The American Stock Exchange

8 Regional Exchanges

Listing Requirements

Trading floor

Specialist/ Open
  Auction System -

Securities Traded

Types of Orders

Market Order
An Order to Buy/Sell at the Best Price When the Order Reaches the Exchange

Buy 1000 WMT
at the Market

Limit Order
An Order to Buy/Sell at a Specified Price

Buy 1000 WMT
at $57 (GTC)

The Financial Markets
Organized Exchanges

Specialist
A Trader Who Makes a Market in One or More Securities and is Charged with Maintaining a Fair and Orderly Market
- Hold Inventory
- Buy/Sell Stock
- Maintain Limit Order Book

Trading Post
Position on Floor Where Specialist Make Markets in Securities

---

NYSE — Leading Specialist Firms

Firm/Ownership	Total Common Stocks	Value by Dollar Value of Specialist Trades	No. of DJIA Stocks	Big Name Stocks
LeBranche & Co. (Publicly traded)	582	26.9%	9	3M; AT&T; Berkshire Hathaway; Delta Airlines
Spear, Leeds, & Kellogg Specialists (unit of Goldman Sachs	573	23.4%	3	Allianz AG; Fannie Mae; FedEx; IBM; MetLife
Fleet Specialists (unit of FleetBoston Financial)	435	20.3%	9	Coca-Cola; Home Depot; GE; GM; McDonald's; Sprint
Van Der Moolen Specialists (publicly traded)	376	10.8%	3	Apache; Cendant; Disney; Harley-Davidson; IDT
Bear Wagner Specialists (minority partner: Bear Stearns	340	15.2%	4	Proctor & Gamble; Citigroup; Deutsche Telekom; Merrill Lynch
Performance Specialist Group (privately held)	139	1.2%	0	CEC Entertainment; Illinois Tool Works; Sony (ADRs); Pep Boys
Susquehanna Specialists (privately held)	122	2.2%	0	Borders Group; IHOP; OfficeMax; Reebok

---

Organized Exchange — The Specialist System

The specialists system is also known as the open auction system

Exchange Floor

Orders → Open Auction ← Orders

Specialist

Trading Post

Orders → ← Orders

Specialist Directly Participates in 15% of Trades

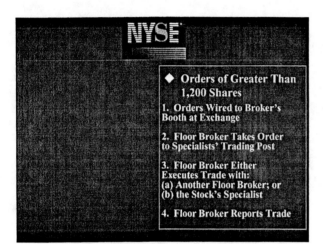

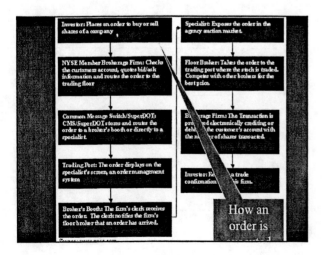

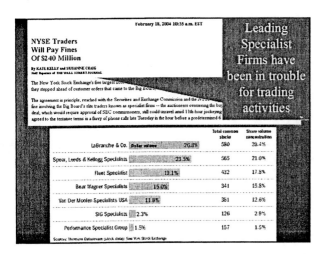

February 18, 2004 10:35 a.m. EST

NYSE Traders
Will Pay Fines
Of $240 Million

By KATE KELLY and SUSANNE CRAIG
Staff Reporters of THE WALL STREET JOURNAL

The New York Stock Exchange's five largest _____
they stepped ahead of customer orders that came to the Big Board _____

The agreement in principle, reached with the Securities and Exchange Commission and the NYSE _____
fine involving the Big Board's elite traders known as specialist firms -- the auctioneers overseeing the buy _____
deal, which would require approval of SEC commissioners, still could unravel amid 11th-hour jockeying _____
agreed to the tentative terms in a flurry of phone calls late Tuesday in the hour before a predetermined 6 _____

Leading Specialist Firms have been in trouble for trading activities

			Total common stocks	Share volume concentration
LaBranche & Co.	Dollar volume	26.8%	580	28.4%
Spear, Leeds & Kellogg Specialists		23.5%	565	21.0%
Fleet Specialist		19.1%	432	17.8%
Bear Wagner Specialists		15.0%	341	15.8%
Van Der Moolen Specialists USA		11.8%	381	12.6%
SIG Specialists		2.3%	126	2.9%
Performance Specialist Group		1.5%	157	1.5%

Sources: Thomson Datastream (stock data); New York Stock Exchange

---

Financial Markets
The Over-The-Counter Market

The OTC Market is known as the Competitive Market Maker System – it is a computer network linking stock brokers and dealers

The Over-the-Counter Market (OTC)

Broker/Dealer System

The Competitive Market Maker System

NASDAQ System

Securities Traded

Financial Markets
The Over-The-Counter Market

Security Dealer
Security Firms Who Makes a Market in One or More Securities Known as Market Makers

NASDAQ
Automated Quotation System Which Provides Dealer Bid and Ask Quotes

Bid Prices
Price at Which Dealer will Buy

Ask Prices
Price at Which Dealer will Sell

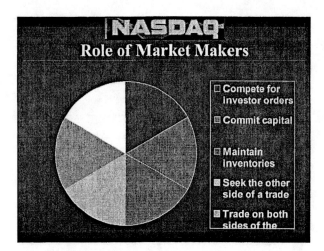

The Anatomy of a Trade

1. Broker Obtains Bid/Ask Quotes on Stock from NASDAQ System

2. Broker Directs Order to Dealer Offering the Best Price
(a) Buy Order - Lowest Ask Price
(b) Sell Order - Highest Bid Price

3. Broker Confirms Trade

KEY: For Buy Order, Broker looks for Dealer with Lowest Ask Price; For Sell Order, Brokers looks for Dealer with Highest Bid Price

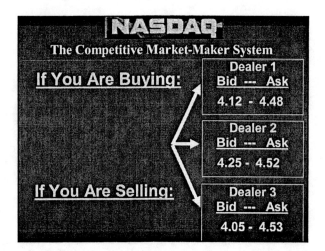

Dealer Markets

Buyers & Sellers Evaluate Bids/Asks from Dealers

	Dealer 1	Dealer 2	Dealer 3	Dealer 4	Dealer 5	Dealer 6
Bid	20.90	20.94	20.91	20.97	20.96	20.93
	800	300	500	200	400	300
Ask	21.15	21.18	21.20	21.17	21.19	21.18
	100	400	500	400	200	300
Spread	.25	.24	.29	.20	.23	.25

Measures of the Stock Market

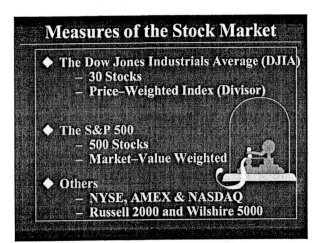

- ◆ The Dow Jones Industrials Average (DJIA)
    - 30 Stocks
    - Price–Weighted Index (Divisor)

- ◆ The S&P 500
    - 500 Stocks
    - Market–Value Weighted

- ◆ Others
    - NYSE, AMEX & NASDAQ
    - Russell 2000 and Wilshire 5000

Measures of the Stock Market

DOWJONES Indexes

3M Company	Eastman Kodak Company	J.P. Morgan Chase & Company
Alcoa Incorporated	Exxon Mobil Corporation	Johnson & Johnson
Altria Group, Incorporated	General Electric Company	McDonald's Corporation
American Express Company	General Motors Corporation	Merck & Company, Incorporated
AT&T Corporation	Hewlett-Packard Company	Microsoft Corporation
Boeing Company	Home Depot Incorporated	Procter & Gamble Company
Caterpillar Incorporated	Honeywell International Inc.	SBC Communications Incorporated
Citigroup Incorporated	Intel Corporation	United Technologies Corporation
Coca-Cola Company	International Business Machines	Wal-Mart Stores Incorporated
DuPont	International Paper Company	Walt Disney Company

Only 30 Stocks
Price Weighted
ATT - $20 — 10% Increase adds 2 points to DJIA
IBM - $100 – 10 % Increase Adds 10 Points to DJIA

Measures of the Stock Market

- Desc	GICS®[1]	NC[2]	MKTCAP[3,4]	Level[5]	(DD-MMM-YYYY) Daily	MTD	QTD	YTD
S&P 500		500	10,5					
Energy	10	23	6					
Materials	15	33	3					
Industrials	20	59	1,1					
Consumer Discretionary	25	87	1,1					
Consumer Staples	30	37	1,1					
Health Care	35	47	1,4					
Financials	40	83	2,2					
Information Technology	45	83	1,8					
Telecommunications Services	50	12	373,327	117.018	(0.22%)	1.38%	5.12%	5.12%
Utilities	55	36	297,075	120.08	0.22%	(0.41%)	1.43%	1.43%

S&P 500
500 Stocks
Market-Value Weights
Model of US Economy
Ten Sectors

Stock Market Measures

DJIA
S&P 500
Russell 2000
NASDAQ

The Market for Common Stock

◆ **Commissions**
  - **Retail**
  - **Discount**
  - **Institutional**

◆ **Daily Volume**

◆ **Market Share of Exchanges & OTC**

Capital Markets
Recent Issues

NYSE Governance

Specialists Versus Market-Makers

Round-the-Clock Trading

Competition Between NYSE, OTC/AMEX, and ECNs and Market Structure

Search for Best Price

The Financial System, Intermediation, and Financial Institutions

---

The Financial System, Intermediation, and Financial Institutions

This module introduces and defines financial intermediaries, and explores the economic role of such institutions. Objectives for this module include:

(1) Understanding the functions of the financial system and the <u>need for financial intermediaries</u> in this system
(2) Explaining the <u>different forms of financial intermediation</u> and how these are exploited by financial institutions;
(3) Provide an evaluation of the <u>different types of financial institutions</u>
(4) Explore the <u>Convergence of Financial Services</u>; and
(5) Discuss <u>Mutual Funds</u> as Financial Intermediaries

The Financial System, Intermediation, and Financial Institutions

1. Financial Intermediation

2. Financial Institutions:
   Balance Sheet/Income Statement

3. The Convergence of Financial Services

Financial Intermediation

Willie Sutton
Famous Bank Robber

Question
Why do You Rob Banks?

Depository Institutions and Securities Markets as Financial Intermediaries

RISING FORCE OF MARKETS
Share of total net credit market lending

*Depository institutions include commercial banks and other institutional lenders.
Note: Other sources include Insurers, pension funds, etc.
Sources: Federal Reserve Board Flow of Funds; Mark Zandi, RFA Dismal Sciences

•There Has Been An Increase In the Popularity of Securities Markets In Providing Financing For Corporations

•Funds Provided By Commercial Banks and Other Institutional Lenders Are On a Decline

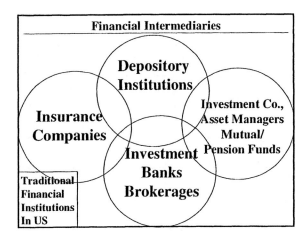

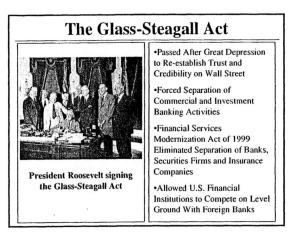

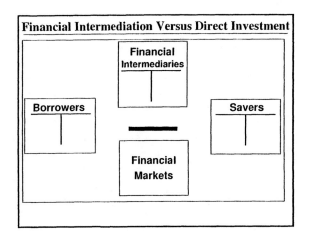

Financial Institutions
Forms of Financial Intermediation

→ Denomination

→ Liquidity and Maturity

→ Default Risk/
   Diversification

→ Economies of Scale in
   Information and
   Transactions Costs

Denomination Intermediation

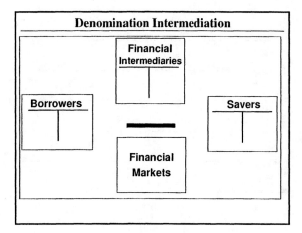

Liquidity/Maturity Intermediation

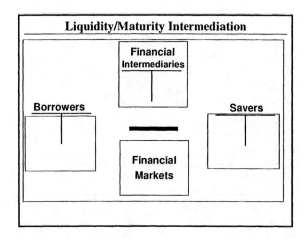

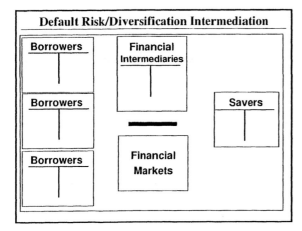

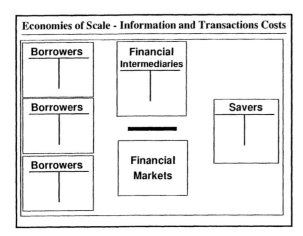

Financial Institutions
Forms of Financial Intermediation

→ Denomination

→ Liquidity and Maturity

→ Default Risk/
Diversification

→ Economies of Scale
in Information and
Transactions Costs

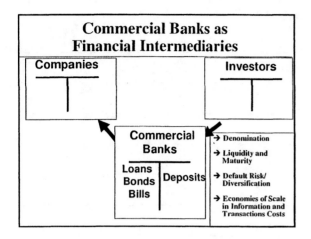

Commercial Banks as Financial Intermediaries

Companies

Investors

Commercial Banks

Loans Bonds Bills | Deposits

→ Denomination
→ Liquidity and Maturity
→ Default Risk/ Diversification
→ Economies of Scale in Information and Transactions Costs

Financial Institutions
Sources and Uses of Funds

Banks		Investment Banks	
Loans	Deposits	Securities	Debt

Insurance		Investment Co.	
Bonds	Reserves	Securities	Shares

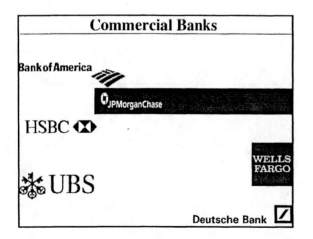

Commercial Banks

Bank of America

JPMorganChase

HSBC

WELLS FARGO

UBS

Deutsche Bank

Twenty Largest US Depository Institutions

	Bank Name	Headquarters	Deposits (billions)	Assets (billions)
1	Bank of America (& Fleet)	Charlotte, NC	$612	$937
2	Citicorp	New York, NY	$474	$1,264
3	JP Morgan Chase	New York, NY	$326	$771
4	Wells Fargo	San Francisco, CA	$248	$388
5	Wachovia	Charlotte, NC	$224	$401
6	Bank One	Columbus, OH	$164	$327
7	Washington Mutual	Seattle, WA	$120	$238
8	U.S. Bancorp	Minneapolis, MN	$119	$189
9	SunTrust Bank	Atlanta, GA	$81.2	$125
10	HSBC Holding	London	$64.5	$93.0
11	National City	Cleveland, OH	$63.5	$114
12	BB&T Corporation	Winston-Salem, NC	$59.3	$90.5
13	Royal Bank of Scotland	Edinburgh	$57.9	$77.7
14	Fifth Third Bancorp	Cincinnati, OH	$57.1	$91.1
15	ABN Amro (LaSalle Bank)	Amsterdam	$57.0	$107
16	Bank of New York	New York, NY	$56.4	$92.4
17	KeyCorp	Cleveland, OH	$50.9	$84.1
18	State Street Corp.	Boston, MA	$47.5	$87.5
19	Golden West World Savings	Oakland, CA	$46.8	$82.0
20	PNC Bank	Pittsburgh, PA	$45.3	$66.2

Investment Banks

MORGAN STANLEY DEAN WITTER

Merrill Lynch · Be Bullish

Goldman Sachs

Charles Schwab

LEHMAN BROTHERS

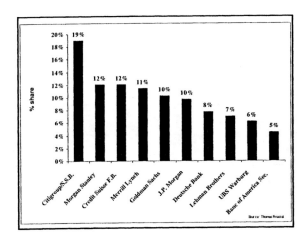

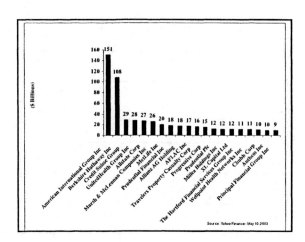

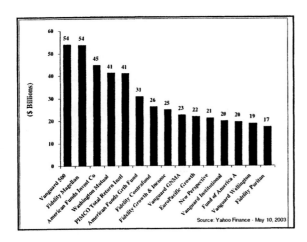

Source: Yahoo Finance - May 10, 2003

The Convergence of Financial Services

Deregulation -
  The Financial Services
  Modernization Act of 1999

Financial Innovation

Globalization and Integration
of Markets

Demographics

Information and
Telecommunications Technologies

Consumer Preferences

$700B in Assets, 100M Customers in 100 Countries, 170,000 Employees

 Travelers Group

1997 Net Profit - $4.5B   1997 Net Profit - $3.4B

| ■ Life Insurance |
| ■ Consumer Finance |
| ■ Property Casualty Insurance |
| □ Salomon Smith Barney |

| ■ Emerging Mkts. In Consumer Bus. |
| ⊞ Developed Mkts |
| ■ Emerging Mkts in Corporate Bus. |
| □ Global Rel. Banking |

Banking, Insurance, Brokerage, Mutual Funds

133

Citigroup Companies:

* Primerica PRIMERICA
* Citibank **citibank**
* Travelers Bank & Trust
* Travelers Life & Annuity **Travelers**
* Travelers Property Casualty
* Salomon Smith Barney SALOMON SMITH BARNEY
* Citigroup Asset Management **citigroup** Asset Management
* CitiFinancial **citi** financial
* Associates
  - On November 30th, 2000, Citigroup officially acquired The Associates

Commercial Banking
Investment Banking and Brokerage
Insurance
Asset Management – Mutual Funds

Chapter 9

The Time Value of Money

Time Value of Money: Compounding and Discounting

Chapter Overview

- 9.1 Compounding and Future Value

- 9.2 Present Value and Discounting

- 9.3 Summary

Compounding and Future Value: Topics to be Examined

How a single investment and multiple investments grow by compounding;

Changing the Compounding Period;

How taxes affect future values on your investments;

Finding Rates of Return.

Time Value of Money: Compounding and Discounting

- **Compounding**-going from a known value today, to an expected but unknown value in the future. Compounding-multiply, over a number of time periods, by number greater than 1.0.

- **Future value**-amount of money an investment will grow to by earning a certain rate of return over time.

Future Value and Compounding: How are they used in Practice?

Estimating your portfolio's future value at the time of your retirement.

Saving funds necessary to finance your child's education.

Estimating a corporation's yearly budget to fund pension payment requirements.

The Cost of Smoking—Money Blown Away

You quit your pack a day habit and invest your savings in a stock mutual fund

How much will you have at age 65?

Assume your current age is 20

Cost per pack is $3

Estimated rate of return is 12% a year

At 65, you expect to have......

$1,487,262

Types of Interest Payments

Simple Interest-interest to be paid only on the original principal invested. The interest is not reinvested. No interest is earned on interest.

Compound Interest-accumulating interest on an investment for more than one period and reinvesting the interest. Interest is earned on interest.

How a Single Investment Grows: Simple Interest

Year	Beginning Balance	Interest Earned	Ending Balance
1	$100.00	$8.00	$108.00
2	$108.00	$8.00	$116.00
3	$116.00	$8.00	$124.00

How a Single Investment Grows: Compound Interest

Year	Beginning Balance	Interest Earned	Ending Balance
1	$100.00	$8.00	$108.00
2	$108.00	$8.64	$116.64
3	$116.64	$9.33	$125.97

How a Single Investment Grows: Compound Interest

Year	Beginning Balance	Interest Earned	Ending Balance
1	$100.00	$8.00	$108.00
2	$108.00	$8.64	$116.64
3	$116.64	$9.33	$125.97

$100 * 1.08 ^ 1 = $108.00

$100 * 1.08 ^ 2 = $116.64

$100 * 1.08 ^ 3 = $125.97

Types of Problems for Single Payment Investments

Future Value of a Single Payment

Calculate the Rate of Return on a Single Payment

Calculate the Initial Payment Needed to have a Required Future Value

---

FV Formula for a Single Payment with Compound Interest

FV = PV * FVSP Factor (r,n)

FV = PV * (1.0 + r)^n

If PV = $100, r = 10%, n = 20 years, then:

FV = $100 * (1.10)^20

FV = $100 * (6.7275) = $672.75

Table 8-3 (Page 8-6) show FVSP info.

Future Value of a Single Payment Investment Using a Financial Calculator

- The five financial function keys, n—number of periods, r or i—interest rate or yield, PV—present value, PMT—periodic payment, and FV—future value
- Example: Nancy wants to invest $5000 today with a bank that promises to pay her 5% per year for 30 years

- Clear your calculator! Inputs are: n = 30, i = 5, PMT = 0, PV = -$5000—the cash outflow, solve for FV, which is equal to $21,609.71

Finding the rate of return on a single payment-FVSP Table 9-3

You invest $125 today

You have $314.77 in 12 years

Find your required rate of return

FV = PV * FVSP Factor (r,n)

$314.77 = $125 * (1+r)^12

(1+r)^12 = 314.77 / 125 = 2.5182

Find the 12-year factor in the Single Payment Table (8-3) closest to 2.5182

It is the 8% factor

Rate of Return on a Single Payment Investment (Calculator)

- Calculate the rate of return on a single investment.

- Thirty years ago, Nancy invested $5000. The investment has grown to $21,609.71. What is Nancy's rate of return?

- Clear your calculator! Inputs are: n = 30, FV = $21,609.71, PMT = 0, PV = -$5000—the cash outflow, solve for i, which is equal to 5%

Finding the initial investment for a Future Value (FVSP Table 9-3)

You need to invest ? Today @ 8% to have $314.77 in 12 years?

Find your required initial investment

FV = PV * FVSP Factor (8,12)

$314.77 = PV * 2.5182

PV = 314.77 / 2.5182 = $125

Calculate the Present Value Payment for a Future Value (Calculator)

- Calculate the initial payment that you need to receive an amount in the future.

- How much should Nancy deposit today at 5% to receive a compounded amount of $21,609.71 in 30 years.

- Inputs are: n = 30, FV = $21,609.71, PMT = 0, r = 5%, solve for PV, which is equal to -$4,999.99.

The Rule of 72 (for single payments)

How long it takes an investment to double in value for a given interest rate. Divide 72 by the interest rate to get the number of years. Not exact.

8%	72 / 8 = 9 years	1.08 ^ 9 = 1.999
6%	72 / 6 = 12 years	1.06 ^ 12 = 2.012
10%	72 / 10 =7.2years	1.10 ^ 7.2 = 1.986

The Compounding Period: How it Affects Future Value

Shortening the compounding period increases the <u>Effective Annual Rate</u>

Annual @ 12% = $100*1.12 = **$112.00**

Semi-annual @ 6% = $100*1.06^2 = **$112.36**

Quarterly @ 3% = $100*1.03^4 = **$112.55**

Monthly @ 1% =$100*1.01^12 = **$112.68**

More frequent compounding is good for investors—higher effective annual rate.

The Effect of Taxes

Interest earned is usually taxable

Suppose your tax rate is 25% and you invest $100 at 8%

Investment	Interest Earned	Taxes	After-taxes
$100	$8	$2	$6

Your after-tax rate of return is **6%**

After-tax rate=Before-tax rate*(1-tax rate)=8% * (1-.25)=6%

An Example of Compounding after Taxes

You invest $250 at 10%

Your tax rate is 40%

How much will you have in 25 years?

After-tax rate = 10% * (1-.40) = 6%

$250 * (1.06 ^ 25) = **$1,073**

Note that if you didn't pay taxes, you would have....

$250 * (1.10 ^ 25) = **$2,709**

Tax -advantaged investing for retirement

401(k) plans....named for paragraph 401(k) of the internal revenue code

Traditional I.R.A. (Individual Retirement Account)

Roth I.R.A.

FV Formula for Multiple Payments with Compound Interest

FV = Payment * FVMP Factor (r,n)

If Payment = $100/year, r = 10%, n = 20 years, then:

FV = $100 * FVMP Factor (10%, 20)

FV = $100 * (57.2750) = $5,727.50

Table 9-4 shows FVMP info.

Types of Problems for Multiple Payment Investments

Future Value of Multiple Payments

Calculate the Rate of Return on Multiple Payments

Calculate the Multiple Payments Needed to have a Required Future Value

Future Value of Multiple Payments

What's the Future Value of investing $1 at the end of each year for four years?

3/15/2006	$1	$1 * 1.08^3 = 1.2597
3/15/2007	$1	$1 * 1.08^2 = 1.1664
3/15/2008	$1	$1 * 1.08^1 = 1.0800
3/15/2009	$1	$1 * 1.08^0 = <u>1.0000</u>

The sum of these is   <u>4.5061</u>

Check your FVMP table at 8%-4 years to see this number

Future Value of Multiple Payments: Practice Problem-no Taxes (Table 9-4)

Your plan is to invest $1,000 a year in a Roth IRA

You expect to earn 10% a year. How much will you have at age 65 if you begin at age 45?

$1,000 * 57.2750 = **$57,275**

Future Value of Multiple Payments: Practice Problem-with Taxes

Your plan is to invest $1,000 a year in a savings account

You expect to earn 10% a year but you will pay income taxes annually at the rate of 40%. How much will you have at age 65 if you begin at age 45?

$1,000 * 36.7856 = **$36,785.60**

Future Value of Multiple Payments Using a Financial Calculator

Nancy wants to invest $5,000 at the end of <u>every year</u> @ 5% per year for 30 years. What is the future value of her investment?

Clear your calculator! Inputs are: n = 30, i = 5, PV = 0, PMT = -$5000 the cash outflows, solve for FV, which equals <u>$332,194.23.</u>

Finding the Rate of return on a Multiple Payment Investments (Table 9-4)`

You invest $125 a year for 10 years
You end up with $2,150
Find your rate of return
$125 * Factor = $2,150
Factor = $2,150 / $125 = 17.2
Look across from 10 years till you find this factor

Answer: Between 10% and 12%

Finding the Rate of Return on a Multiple Payment Investments (Calculator)

You invest $125 a year for 10 years and end up with $2,150. Find your rate of return

Calculator inputs: PMT = -$125, PV = 0, n = 10, FV = $2,150, find i;

Rate of Return i = <u>11.58%</u>

Chapter 10

Discounted Cash Flow Valuation

Discounted Cash Flow Valuation

Chapter Objectives

- **Learn to calculate future and present value of level cash flow streams and uneven cash flow streams**

- **Learn to calculate loan payments, effective interest rates, and amortization schedules**

- **Learn to value stocks and bonds using the DCF approach**

Discounted Cash Flow Valuation

Chapter Overview

- **10.1 Introduction to DCF Valuation**

- **10.2 Valuing Level Cash Flows**

- **10.3 Valuing Uneven Cash Flows**

- **10.4 Summary**

Introduction to DCF Valuation

- **DCF determines the** *value* **of an investment.**
- **The markets determine the** *price* **of an investment.**
- **You decide, based on price or cost, if the investment is undervalued, overvalued, or fairly-valued.**
- **Your buy/sell decision should be based** solely **on** *price versus value*.

Introduction to DCF Valuation-Definitions

- **The** *value* **of an investment (stock, bond, mortgage, etc.) equals the present value of its expected cash flows, discounted (reduced) for their risk and timing.**

- *Expected cash flows* **are the most likely cash payments (dividends, interest, capital gain or loss) that you can expect (not hope) to receive.**

Introduction to DCF Valuation- Definitions

- *Discount:* **multiply a number by less than one.**
- *Discount rate*: **a function of time and risk:** **discount rate = f (time, risk)**
- *Discount factor:* **a function of both time and the discount rate- [discount factor = f (time, discount rate)]**
- *Present value (PV)* **of an investment is the sum of the expected cash flows multiplied by their respective discount factors**

Introduction to DCF Valuation: Loans

- *Level cash flows*: the interest rate and cash flows associated with the loans, mortgages, and annuities are fixed and do not change;

- A *loan* is an obligation under which a person borrows money from a lender;

- *Terms* of the loan state an interest rate and a repayment or *amortization schedule*.

Introduction to DCF Valuation: Mortgages

- Home mortgage: an obligation under which a person borrows money from a bank and uses the proceeds to purchase a house or condominium.

- Amortization schedule: Level payments over a long time period, usually 20 to 30 years.

Introduction to DCF Valuation: Annuities

- An *life annuity* is contract sold by pension funds and life insurance companies;

- Pays a specified amount of money per year to owner;

- Amortization schedule more complex than loans or mortgage.

- Investor makes a single payment or multiple payments then withdraws funds upon her retirement.

Introduction to DCF Valuation: Mortgage Example- (Table 8-7)

- **Gary borrows $100,000 from a bank at 8% and 25 year mortgage. What is his annual payment?**
  - n = 25 years, PV = $100,000, r or i = 8%, FV = 0
  - PV = PMT * PVMP Factor (25, 8%)
  - $100,000 = PMT * 10.6748
  - $100,000/10.6748 = PMT
  - PMT = -$9,368/year
  - Total Payments = 25 * -$9,368 = -$234,197
  - Interest = -$134,197, Principal Repayment = -$100,000

Introduction to DCF Valuation: Mortgage Example-Rates up 2% to 10%

- **Interest rates on mortgages increase by 2% to 10%, what is Gary's annual payment on a 10% loan?**
  - n = 25 years, PV = $ 100,000, r or i = 10%, FV = 0
  - PV = PMT * PVMP Factor (25, 10%)
  - $100,000 = PMT * 9.0770
  - $100,000/9.0770 = PMT
  - PMT = -$10,608/year
  - Total Payments = 25 * -$10,608 = $265,200
  - Interest = -$165,200, Principal Repayment = -$100,000

Introduction to DCF Valuation: Mortgage Example-Rates drop 2% to 6%

- **If interest rates on mortgages decrease by 2% to 6%, what is Gary's annual payment on a 6% loan?**
  - n = 25 years, PV = $ 100,000, r or i = 6%, FV = 0
  - PV = PMT * PVMP Factor (25, 6%)
  - $100,000 = PMT * 12.7834
  - $100,000/12.7834 = PMT
  - PMT = -$7,823/year
  - Total Payments = 25 * -$7,823 = $195,567
  - Interest = -$95,567, Principal Repayment = -$100,000

Introduction to DCF Valuation: The Three-Step Approach

1. Develop a set of *expected cash flows*;
2. Estimate the *discount rate* and calculate the discount factors;
3. Multiply the cash flows by the discount factors and add them to determine the *value* of the asset.

Decision Rule:
- If the *value* of an asset is *greater* than its *price*—Buy it!
- If the *value* is *less* than its *price*—Sell it!

Valuing Level Cash Flows: Amortizing a loan

- Example: Randy likes fast women, Budweiser and expensive cars. He wants to buy a BMW for $50,000? He can finance it with a bank loan at 10% for 4 years. His annual payment is $15,774. What is his *amortization schedule*?

					Interest Rate		10.00%
					Discount Rate		10.00%
	Beginning	Interest	Principal	Annual	Discount		Ending
Year	Principal	Payment	Payment	Payment	Factor	DCF	Principal
1	$50,000	$5,000	$10,774	$15,774	0.9091	$14,340	$39,226
2	$39,226	$3,923	$11,851	$15,774	0.8264	$13,036	$27,375
3	$27,375	$2,737	$13,037	$15,774	0.7513	$11,851	$14,338
4	$14,338	$1,434	$14,340	$15,774	0.683	$10,774	
Totals		$13,094	$50,002	$63,096		$50,001	

Valuing Level Cash Flows- Spreadsheet

- An Excel Spreadsheet makes the DCF calculation easy. Assume interest rates on similar car loans increase to 11%. What's Randy's 10% loan now worth.
- Discount the cash flows now at 11%. Plug 11% into the discount rate slot and the DCF value of Randy's $50,000 car loan is $48,938.

					Interest Rate		10.00%
					Discount Rate		11.00%
	Beginning	Interest	Principal	Annual	Discount		Ending
Year	Principal	Payment	Payment	Payment	Factor	DCF	Principal
1	$50,000	$5,000	$10,774	$15,774	0.9009	$14,211	$39,226
2	$39,226	$3,923	$11,851	$15,774	0.8116	$12,803	$27,375
3	$27,375	$2,737	$13,037	$15,774	0.7312	$11,534	$14,338
4	$14,338	$1,434	$14,340	$15,774	0.6587	$10,391	
Totals		$13,004	$50,002	$63,006		$48,939	

Valuing Level Cash Flows- Calculator

- **Using a financial calculator for PV: Five financial function keys: n—number of periods, r or i—interest rate or yield, PV—present value, PMT—payment, and FV—future value**

- **Randy's Car Loan—Valuing a four-year, 10% loan with a payment of -$15,773.54, discounted @ 11%.**

- **Inputs are: n = 4, i = 11, FV = 0, PMT = -$15,773.54, solve for PV, which is equal to $48,936.55**

Valuing Uneven Cash Flows-Projects

- **Most real world investments such as** projects, stocks and bonds **do not have a single cash flow or level expected cash flows.**

- **A _project_ or venture is an investment to produce a product or provide a service that will generate money in the future.**

- **_Cash Inflows_- additional revenues coming into the company as a result of the project.**

- **_Cash Outflows_- additional expenses being spent by the company as a result of the project.**

Valuing Uneven Cash Flows-Bonds

- **A _bond_ is a debt instrument. Corporations, the US Government, and municipalities issue bonds.**

- **Bonds are payable from taxes from US government or the general revenues of a corporation.**

- **_Cash inflows_ to an investor are bond interest payments, usually every 6 months, and repayment of principal.**

Valuing Uneven Cash Flows-Stocks

- A _stock_ represents ownership interest in a corporation.

- The _cash inflows_ consist of dividends and increase (or decrease) in stock price.

- There is no maturity associated with a stock—the life of a stock is infinite.

- The risk of a stock is hard to quantify, making it difficult to determine the proper discounting rate.

Valuing Uneven Cash Flows Using a Calculator

- Most popular financial calculators have their own specific systems for entering uneven sequential cash flows, and then discounting those cash flows at a uniform discount rate

- HP-12C model:
  - First input the number of periods and press the n button.
  - Then input the discounting rate and press the i button.
  - Then enter cash flow, press the blue _g_ button, and press the _CFj_ button. Use Nj button for equal cash flows.
  - Press the yellow _f_ button and then press the _NPV_ button to calculate the discounted present value for the cash flows

Valuing Uneven Cash Flows of a Project-Using a Spreadsheet

- Bill wants to invest in new machinery to increase paper production and revenues by $3,000,000 per year initially.
- Cost of pulp and additional raw material for the project is $2,500,000 per year. Additional O&M expense of the project will be $100,000 per year.
- Bill estimates revenues will increase at the rate of 6% per year and that costs will increase at a lower rate of 4% per year. The machinery is expected to last 8 years and have no salvage value at the end of this period.
- Projects of similar risk have a discounting rate of 14%.
- How much is this project worth?

151

9.3 Valuing Uneven Cash Flows Using a Spreadsheet   Lemont Paper Project

What do we know? N = 8 years, r = 14%, initial cash inflow is $3,000,000 and increases 6% per year, initial cash outflow is $2,600,00 and increases 4% per year.

Year	Cash Inflow	Cash Outflow	Net Cash Flow	Discount Factor	DCF
			Discount Rate =		14%
1	$3,000	($2,600)	$400	0.8772	$351
2	$3,180	($2,704)	$476	0.7695	$366
3	$3,371	($2,812)	$559	0.675	$377
4	$3,573	($2,925)	$648	0.5921	$384
5	$3,787	($3,042)	$746	0.5194	$387
6	$4,015	($3,163)	$851	0.4556	$388
7	$4,256	($3,290)	$966	0.3996	$386
8	$4,511	($3,421)	$1,089	0.3506	$382
Total			$5,735		$3,021

Valuing Uneven Cash Flows of a Bond Using   a Spreadsheet

- Assume that the U.S. Government has issued a Bond with an 8% interest rate, five-years to the maturity of the Bond, and a principal payment of $1,000.

- The Bond pays interest in the amount of $40 dollars (equal to $1,000 * 8% * ½ year) two times per year (April 1 and October 1), plus the $1,000 repayment of the principal at maturity.

- Also assume that the interest rate associated with this type of bond has increased to 10% in today's market.

- What is the current value of this 8% Bond?

Valuing Uneven Cash Flows of a Bond Using   a Spreadsheet

Period	Cash Flow	Discount Factor	DCF
	Semi Annual Rate =		5%
1	40	0.9524	38.1
2	40	0.907	36.28
3	40	0.8638	34.55
4	40	0.8227	32.91
5	40	0.7835	31.34
6	40	0.7462	29.85
7	40	0.7107	28.43
8	40	0.6768	27.07
9	40	0.6446	25.78
10	1040	0.6139	638.47
Total	$1,400.00		$922.78

Valuing Uneven Cash Flows of a Stock Using a Spreadsheet

- **Valuing a stock involves the same analysis as valuing a fixed-rate mortgage loan, or the U.S. Government Bond.**
- **However, in estimating future cash flows there are two important exceptions:**
  - The Bond and the mortgage have *cash flows that are known with certainty*, while the range of future cash flows for a stock can be enormous.
  - Common stock represents ownership in a corporation, which has an *infinite life* unlike bonds and mortgages

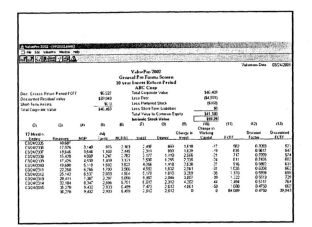

Chapter 11

Capital Budgeting and Measures of Investment Return

Capital Budgeting and Measures of Investment Return

Chapter Objectives

- Learn the process of capital budgeting and estimation of incremental cash costs and benefits

- Learn the standard techniques for measuring investment returns relating to capital budgeting problems

- Understand the contribution of capital budgeting towards increasing stock prices of a company and maximizing shareholder value

---

Capital Budgeting and Measures of Investment Return

Chapter Overview

- 11.1   Capital Budgeting
- 11.2   Net Present Value
- 11.3   Internal Rate of Return
- 11.4   Other Measures Relating to Capital Budgeting
    - Payback Period
    - Book Rate of Return
    - Profitability Index

Capital Budgeting and Measures of Investment Return

11.1   Capital Budgeting

- **Capital budgeting-process of planning and managing a firm's long-term investment in projects and ventures**
- **Capital Budgeting involves estimating the** *amount, timing, and risk of future cash flows*
- **Capital budgeting:**
  - starts with estimation of incremental cash flows from a project;
  - create a time line of expected cash flows; and
  - compare the present value of the cash flows with cost of project

---

Capital Budgeting and Measures of Investment Return

11.2   Net Present Value (NPV)

- **NPV of an investment-difference between the value and cost of investment.**

- **The value of any project is equal to the present value of its expected cash flows, discounted for risk and timing.**

- **NPV Rule-invest in projects if NPV is positive. Reject if NPV is negative**

Capital Budgeting and Measures of Investment Return

Net Present Value Example

Textile Inc is considering buying a new machine. The machine requires an initial outlay of $250,000 and is expected to generate incremental cash inflows of $120,000 for the next 5 years and requires $30,000 yearly cash outflows for maintenance. At the end of five years, the machine will have no disposable value. Calculate the Net Present Value of the project if the discount rate is 15% per year

Capital Budgeting and Measures of Investment Return

Procedure for solving the NPV Problem
1. Estimate cash flows from the new machine

Year	0	1	2	3	4	5
Inflows	-	120	120	120	120	120
Outflows	(250)	(30)	(30)	(30)	(30)	(30)
Net Cash Flows	(250)	90	90	90	90	90

Capital Budgeting and Measures of Investment Return

Procedure for solving the NPV Problem
2. Calculate the discounted cash flows

Year	0	1	2	3	4	5
Net	(250)	90	90	90	90	90
PV Factor (*)	1.000	0.870	0.756	0.658	0.572	0.497
Discounted Cash Flow	(250)	78.26	68.05	59.18	51.46	44.75

(*) PV Factor = $1/(1 + r)^t$

Capital Budgeting and Measures of Investment Return

Procedure for solving the NPV Problem
3. Calculate NPV and make the decision based on NPV Rule

Year	0	1	2	3	4	5
Discounted Cash Flow	(250)	78.26	68.05	59.18	51.46	44.75
NPV	51.69					
NPV is positive—Invest in the machine						

Capital Budgeting and Measures of Investment Return

11.3 Internal Rate of Return (IRR)

- IRR-rate of return expected to be earned on a project.

- IRR-discounting rate that makes the net present value of an investment equal to zero

- IRR Rule as an investment criterion:
    - if the investment has IRR that is higher than some pre-determined required rate of return, accept investment.
    - if the IRR is lower than required rate of return, reject.

Capital Budgeting and Measures of Investment Return

Internal Rate of Return Example

- Let us continue with the same example of Textile Inc.

    Textile Inc is considering buying a new machine for spinning. The machine requires an initial outlay of $250,000 and is expected to generate incremental cash inflows of $120,000 for the next 5 years and requires $30,000 yearly cash outflows for maintenance. At the end of five years, the machine will have no disposable value. Calculate the IRR of the project

---

Capital Budgeting and Measures of Investment Return

Procedure for solving the IRR

1. Estimate NPV from the machine based on a discount rate. In our case let us start with 15% per year

Year	0	1	2	3	4	5
Net Cash Flows	(250)	90	90	90	90	90
PV Factor	1.000	0.870	0.756	0.658	0.572	0.497
Discounted Cash Flow	(250)	78.26	68.05	59.18	51.46	44.75
NPV			51.69			

Capital Budgeting and Measures of Investment Return

Procedure for solving the IRR

2. Since the NPV calculated at step 1 is positive we increase the discount rate because IRR is the rate at which NPV of the project is 0. Now we take a discount rate of 25% per year

Year	0	1	2	3	4	5
Cash Flows	(250)	90	90	90	90	90
PV Factor	1.000	0.800	0.640	0.512	0.410	0.328
Discounted Cash Flow	(250)	72.00	57.60	46.08	36.86	29.49
NPV			(7.96)			

Capital Budgeting and Measures of Investment Return

Procedure for solving the IRR

3. We continue the process till we find the rate at which NPV is 0. In this example a discount rate of 23.44% gives an NPV of 0 and hence IRR is 23.44% per year

Year	0	1	2	3	4	5
Cash Flows	(250)	90	90	90	90	90
PV Factor	1.000	0.810	0.656	0.532	0.431	0.349
Discounted Cash Flow	(250)	72.91	59.07	47.85	38.76	31.40
NPV			0			

Capital Budgeting and Measures of Investment Return

Procedure for solving the IRR

4. We now compare the IRR calculated with a pre-determined required rate of return and apply the IRR rule to make the decision.

IRR of 23.44% is greater than the required rate of return of 15% per year—Invest in the new machine

Capital Budgeting and Measures of Investment Return

11.4 Other Measures – Payback Period

- Payback period-length of time for the return on an investment takes to cover the cost of the investment.
- Payback period-involves only gross cash flows and not discounted cash flows.
- Payback rule as an investment criterion:
    - accept the investment if its payback period is less than a predetermined number of years;
    - reject the investment if its payback period is greater than the predetermined number of years.

Capital Budgeting and Measures of Investment Return

Payback Period Example

- Tools Inc plans to invest in a new machinery that is expected to cost $100,000. The new machine will generate cash flows of $20,000 every year. Calculate the pay back period

Payback period = 100,000/20,000 = 5 years

If the company has a pre-determined payback period that is higher than the estimated payback period then accept the project, otherwise reject the project

---

Capital Budgeting and Measures of Investment Return

11.4 Other Measures – Book Rate of Return

- Book Rate of Return-an accounting ratio calculated by dividing the company's accounting profits by the book value of the company's assets.
- Book rate of return rule as an investment criterion:
    - accept the investment if its book rate of return exceeds a predetermined target book return;
    - reject the investment if its book rate of return is less than a target book return.

Capital Budgeting and Measures of Investment Return

Book Rate of Return Problem

Continuing with Tools Inc problem and given that Tools Inc. will depreciate the machine fully over the five year period. Calculate the book rate of return

Book Value (Beg)	Income	Book Rate of Return
100,000	20,000	20,000/100,000 = 20%
80,000	20,000	20,000/ 80,000 = 25%
60,000	20,000	20,000/ 60,000 = 33%
40,000	20,000	20,000/ 40,000 = 50%
20,000	20,000	20,000/ 20,000 = 100%

Capital Budgeting and Measures of Investment Return

11.4 Other Measures – Profitability Index (PI)

- PI- The NPV of an investment, divided by its cost.
- PI is used to identify projects that will receive the best return associated with the amount of dollars invested by ranking the projects by PI
- PI rule is:
  - accept the venture with the highest profitability index first;
  - then accept ventures with lower and lower positive PI's until the projects expend the capital budget;
  - do not accept projects with a negative PI.

Capital Budgeting and Measures of Investment Return

Profitability Index Problem

Calculate the profitability Index for the 3 projects given below:

Project	PV	Cost	NPV	Profitability Index
1	5,000	4,200	800	800/4,200 = 0.19
2	2,500	2,000	500	500/2,000 = 0.25
3	3,000	2,700	300	300/2,700 = 0.11

Based on Profitability Index Project 2 will be chosen first, followed by project 1 and then by project 3

Chapter 12

Risk and Return and the Capital Asset Pricing Model

An Important Principle of Finance: CAPM-The Trade-Off Between Return and Risk

Trade-off between the expected return on an investment and its risk.

Low risk Treasury Bills have lower expected returns (2-4%). Stocks (large price volatility) have higher expected returns (e.g. 6-10%).

Risk measured by price or return volatility. More price/return movement—greater risk.

A rational investor requires a higher expected return to accept additional risk.

Model that describes this trade-off is the CAPM.

Risk and Return and the Capital Asset Pricing Model

Risk Return Relationship

Direct tradeoff between the expected rate of return and risk. Tradeoff represented by the diagonal line.

Risk and Return and the Capital Asset Pricing Model

12.3 Historic Returns by Asset Class

Historically, lower risk investments have lower returns and higher risk investments have higher returns! Ibbotson and Sinquefield study

	Return	Std Deviation
Treasury Bills	3.8%	3.2%
Government Bonds	5.3%	9.4%
Corporate Bonds	5.8%	8.6%
Large Company Stock	10.7%	20.2%
Small Company Stock	12.5%	33.2%

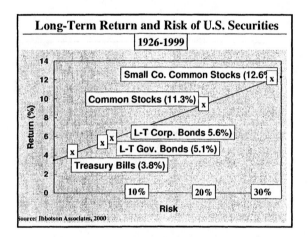

Long-Term Return and Risk of U.S. Securities

1926-1999

Source: Ibbotson Associates, 2000

What is Rate of Return?

Rate of Return = (Cash Payment + Change in Price)/Price Paid;

Buy IBM @ $90, receive a cash dividend of $4, and sell it one year later at $104;

Rate of Return = ($4 + $14) / ($90) = .2 = 20%

Components of Rate of Return

Cash Payments-Dividends and Interest taxed as ordinary income (i.e. up to 35%):

  Dividends- quarterly payments made on some stocks (ownership)

  Interest- semi-annual payments made on bonds (debt)

Change in Price- Capital Gain or Capital Loss

  Realized- you sell your asset and incur gain or loss;
    Unrealized- you continue to own your asset

  If realized, the gains or losses are taxed

    Long-term gains and losses are taxed at a lower rate (e.g. 20%)

    Short-term gains and losses taxed at a higher rate (e.g.

What do we mean by Risk?

Risk-measured by the possible range of returns around an expected return;

Measured by a statistic called the standard deviation of returns;

Risk has both negative and positive outcomes. Generates returns that are lower than expected or higher than expected.

Risk and Return and the Capital Asset Pricing Model

12.2 Definitions Relating to Return and Risk

Standard Deviation of Return - (σ):

- Risk on an asset is measured by the variability of returns

- Standard deviation is the statistic that is that measures how wildly or tightly observed stock returns cluster around the average stock return

- Greater standard deviation means more fluctuations and greater risk

Risk and Return and the Capital Asset Pricing Model

12.2 Definitions Relating to Return and Risk

Calculation of Standard Deviation of Return - (σ):

Example
- The annual returns of stock of XYZ Inc. for the last three years was:

Year 1 – 8%

Year 2 – (1%)

Year 3 – 2%

Risk and Return and the Capital Asset Pricing Model

12.2 Definitions Relating to Return and Risk Calculation of Standard Deviation of Return - (σ):

Step 1 - Take the simple average return of the distribution of returns

Year	Return	Average Return		
1	8%	3%		
2	(1%)	3%		
3	2%	3%		
Total	9%			

Risk and Return and the Capital Asset Pricing Model

12.2 Definitions Relating to Return and Risk Calculation of Standard Deviation of Return - (σ):

Step 2 - Take each individual observed return and subtract the average of the returns

Year	Return	Average Return	Deviation of Return	
1	8%	3%	5%	
2	(1%)	3%	(4%)	
3	2%	3%	(1%)	
Total	9%			

Risk and Return and the Capital Asset Pricing Model

12.2 Definitions Relating to Return and Risk

Calculation of Standard Deviation of Return - (σ):

Step 3 - Square the resulting difference, and add the squares to get the sum of the squares

Year	Return	Average Return	Deviation of Return	Squared Deviation
1	8%	3%	5%	0.0025
2	(1%)	3%	(4%)	0.0016
3	2%	3%	(1%)	0.0001
Total	9%			0.0042

Risk and Return and the Capital Asset Pricing Model

12.2 Definitions Relating to Return and Risk

Calculation of Standard Deviation of Return - (σ):

Step 4 - Divide the sum of the squares by (the total number of observations minus 1)—the result is the _variance_ of the distribution

Variance = 0.0042/(3-1) = 0.0021

Step 5 - The square root of the variance is the standard deviation of the returns

Standard Deviation = 0.0021 ^ 1/2 = 4.58%

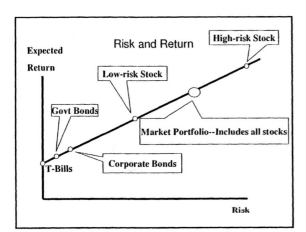

165

Capital Asset Pricing Model (CAPM)

From the Risk-Return Line, we can estimate the expected return on a stock, $E(R_i)$;

Expected return on stock (i), $E(R_i)$ equals the Risk-Free Rate (R_f) + the stock's Beta (β_i) times the Market Risk Premium—the return on the market (R_m) minus (R_f).

$$E(R_i) = R_f + \beta_i * (R_m - R_f)$$

Sample Averages for Investments

		Risk Premium
Treasury Bills	4%	----
Government Bonds	5%	1%
Corporate Bonds	6%	2%
Average Common Stock	12%	8%

Our Questions For Today

How do we measure risk of an asset?

Answer: Beta

What's the relation between beta and return?

Answer: It's very positive

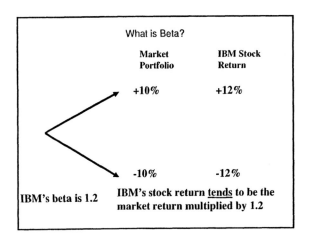

What is Beta?

Market Portfolio	IBM Stock Return
+10%	+12%
-10%	-12%

IBM's beta is 1.2   **IBM's stock return <u>tends</u> to be the market return multiplied by 1.2**

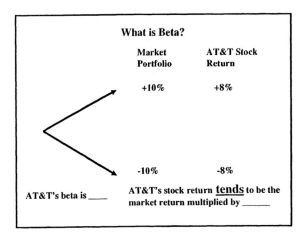

What is Beta?

Market Portfolio	AT&T Stock Return
+10%	+8%
-10%	-8%

AT&T's beta is _____   **AT&T's stock return tends to be the market return multiplied by _____**

A Quick Quiz on Beta

Firm	Market up 20%	Market down 20%	Firm's Beta
Intel	30%	-30%	1.50
GE	15%	-15%	0.75
Apple	20%	-20%	1.00

Why is beta a measure of "Market Magnification"?

A stock with a beta of 2 will tend to double market movements (up or down)

A stock with a beta of 0.50 will tend to have movements (up or down) equal to ½ the market

---

Isn't there more to Risk than Beta?

Yes. <u>Unsystematic</u> or <u>firm specific risk</u>—risk that affects the return of that firm or industry only.

<u>On average, the firm specific risks average out to be zero</u>, if an investor holds a diversified portfolio.

Finance theory assumes that investors are rational and own diversified portfolios.

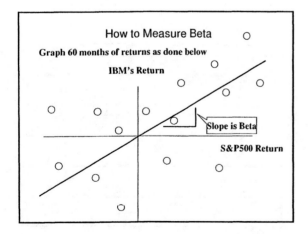

Using Beta to determine Expected Returns

What is a risk premium?
    The amount by which an investment is
expected to outperform T-Bills.

The Market has averaged 12% a year

T-Bills have averaged 4% a year

The market risk premium is 8%   ?

An investment's beta determines its risk premium

T-Bill Rate: 4%
Expected return on Market: 8%
Market risk-premium= 4%
AOL has a beta of 1.6
AOL's risk-premium = 1.6 * 4% = 6.4%
AOL's expected return = 4% + 6.4% = 10.4%

An investment's beta determines its risk premium

T-Bill Rate: 4%
Expected return on Market: 8%
Market risk-premium= 4%
ATT has a beta of 0.6
ATT's risk-premium = 0.6 * 4% = 2.4%
ATT's expected return = 4% + 2.4% = 6.4%

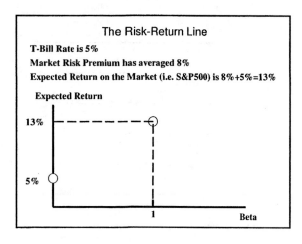

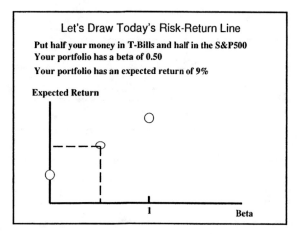

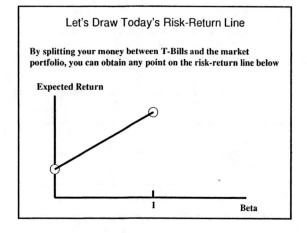

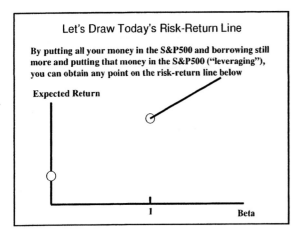

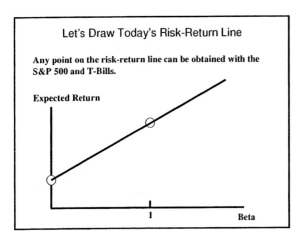

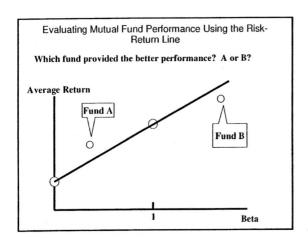

"Alpha" measures performance

A positive alpha is good....a negative alpha is not so good

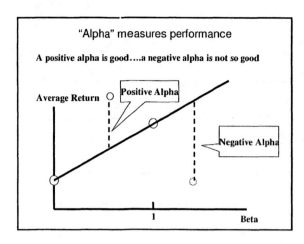

"Alpha" measures performance

Remember, the Risk-Return line is also called the zero-talent line so performance below the line is poor

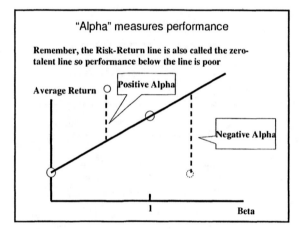

Practice Problem

T-Bills averaged 4% over last few years

S&P 500 averaged 14%

The XYZ Fund had an average return of 16% and a beta of 1.4

Find XYZ's alpha

The CAPM risk-return line for a beta of 1.4 is at   4% + [1.4 * 10%] = 18%

XYZ's alpha is 16%-18% = -2%

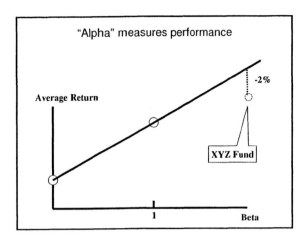

"Alpha" measures performance

Average Return

-2%

XYZ Fund

1   Beta

Practice Problem

T-Bills averaged 4% over last few years

S&P500 averaged 14%

The Nittany Lion Fund had an average return of 16% and a beta of 0.80

Find Nittany Lion's alpha

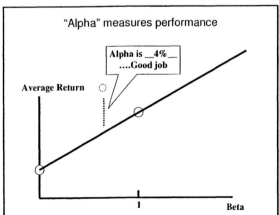

"Alpha" measures performance

Average Return

Alpha is __4%__
....Good job

1   Beta

Chapter 13

Efficient Capital Markets and Random Walks

Review of Some Definitions

$\underline{CAPM} = E(R_i) = R_f + \beta_i * (R_m - R_f)$

$\underline{\text{Market Risk Premium}} = (R_m - R_f)$

$\underline{\text{Beta}} = \text{Risk} = \beta_i = [E(R_i) - R_f] / (R_m - R_f)$

$\underline{\text{Alpha}}$ = Observed Return of Asset – Expected Return of Asset

$\underline{\text{Unsystematic Risk}}$ or firm specific risk- the risk that can be diversified away

$\underline{\text{Systematic Risk}}$- market related risk as measured by Beta. Can not be diversified away

---

Practice Problem

T-Bills averaged 5% over last few years

S&P 500 averaged 15%

The ABC Fund had an average return of 14% and a beta of 0.80

<u>What's the fund's expected return?</u>

CAPM Equation: $E(R_i) = R_f + \beta_i * (R_m - R_f)$

Expected Return = 5% + .8(15% - 5%) = <u>13%</u>

<u>Find ABC's alpha</u>

Alpha = Observed Return – Expected Return

Alpha = 14% - 13% = 1%

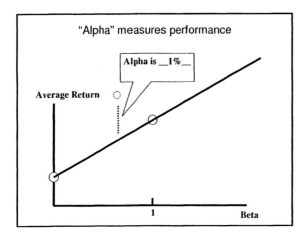

"Alpha" measures performance

Alpha is __1%__

Average Return

1

Beta

Alpha Applied to Mutual Funds

Gross Return means "before expenses"
Net Return = Gross Return - Expenses

For XYZ, gross return = 11.4%

For XYZ, expense ratio is 1.2%
(about average for stock funds)

What is XYZ's net return?

Net Return = 11.4% - 1.2% = 10.2%

Mutual Fund Performance
Use this information for your own investing

Using gross returns, the average fund has an alpha of 0%

What is the average alpha using net returns?

-1.2%

Is good performance in the past (using gross returns) an indicator of good future performance?

NO!!

89% of funds failed to match the S&P500 over the past 5 years

Index Funds are hard to beat

A good practice question

The XYZ fund had a positive alpha using gross returns over the past five years. What is its expected alpha using gross returns for the next five years?

Answer: 0%

Using net returns?
Negative the amount of expenses

An Important Principle of Finance:
Efficient Capital Markets

Asset prices react very quickly to the receipt of new information.

New information is random. Can be good or bad.

Quick reaction of many market participants to new information tends to drive prices to their "correct" level.

What is an
"EFFICIENT MARKET"?

A market where all investments are accurately priced

This means there are no good investments

Also, there are no bad investments

Each investment offers an expected return to match its level of risk

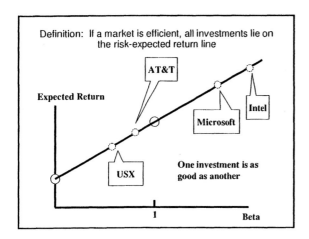

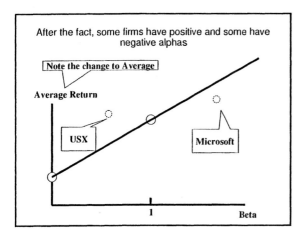

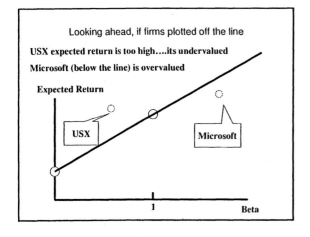

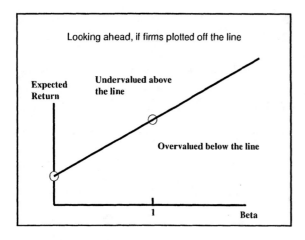

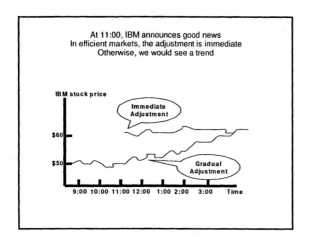

Efficient Capital Markets and Random Walks

Random Walk Hypothesis:

▪ A <u>Random Walk</u> **is a path a variable takes where the future direction of the path (up or down) can't be predicted solely on the basis of past movements.**

▪ **If stock markets are efficient, share prices react immediately to news. There is no   predictable trend implied by a gradual. In an efficient market, share price changes are** <u>random</u>

Efficient Capital Markets and Random Walks

13.2 Types of Market Efficiency

Weak form efficiency- **stock prices reflect the information contained in the history of past stock prices and trading volume.**
- **Implies daily stock price changes are independent;**
- **Useless to try to detect and exploit trends in stock prices.**

Efficient Capital Markets and Random Walks

13.2 Types of Market Efficiency

Semi-strong form efficiency- **stock prices reflect all publicly available information.**
- **Implies stock prices react quickly to new info and prevents investors from earning abnormal returns.**

Efficient Capital Markets and Random Walks

13.2 Types of Market Efficiency

Strong-form efficiency- **stock prices reflect all information, including information not available to the investment community.**

Efficient Capital Markets and Random Walks

13.3 Tests of Market Efficiency

▪ Goal of many of the studies is to find investment strategy that produces investment returns greater than a long-term buy-and-hold strategy for a diversified portfolio of stocks.

▪ The majority of studies have shown that new information is quickly incorporated into stock prices. The excess returns arbitraged away and that stock market is relatively efficient, or at least semi-efficient.

Efficient Capital Markets and Random Walks

13.3 Tests of Market Efficiency

Behavioral Finance:

▪ Academicians who specialize in the field of behavioral finance, have challenged Modern Portfolio Theory's assumption that investors are rational and markets behave rationally.

▪ Behavioral theorists have conducted studies that show that stock markets were not efficient and people and markets, at times, behave irrationally.

Efficient Capital Markets and Random Walks

13.3 Tests of Market Efficiency

The Fama and French Study:

▪ Fama and French study compares the performance of the returns associated with portfolios of stocks that have certain similar characteristics

▪ The study showed, among other things, portfolios of stock with a high book value (BE) to market value (ME) ratio consistently outperformed portfolios with low (BE/ME) ratios and called to question the validity of efficient capital markets

Markets may not be all that efficient!

Portfolio	Monthly Return	Annualized Return	Avg. Number of Stocks	Weighted Avg. Return	Difference in Return
1A	0.30%	3.60%	89	14.99%	-11.39%
1B	0.67%	8.04%	98	14.99%	-6.95%
2	0.87%	10.44%	209	14.99%	-4.55%
3	0.97%	11.64%	222	14.99%	-3.35%
4	1.04%	12.48%	226	14.99%	-2.51%
5	1.17%	14.04%	230	14.99%	-0.95%
6	1.30%	15.60%	235	14.99%	0.61%
7	1.44%	17.28%	237	14.99%	2.29%
8	1.50%	18.00%	239	14.99%	3.01%
9	1.59%	19.08%	239	14.99%	4.09%
10A	1.92%	23.04%	120	14.99%	8.05%
10B	1.83%	21.96%	117	14.99%	6.97%
			2261		

1992 Fama and French Stock Return Study
Portfolios Based on Ascending Book Equity/Market Equity Ratios

---

F&F Study shows interesting anomaly

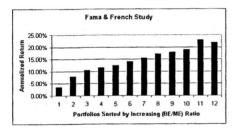

Fama & French Study

Efficient Capital Markets and Random Walks

13.3 Tests of Market Efficiency

The Fama and French Study (Contd.):

- Finds that stocks with high p/e ratios outperform stocks with low p/e ratios;
- Stocks with small market caps outperform stocks with large market caps.
- Other researchers find roughly the same results.

Efficient Capital Markets and Random Walks

13.3 Tests of Market Efficiency

   Less Technical Evidence from the Real World:

- Evidence indicates stock price changes are independent.
- Evidence indicates stock prices react quickly to news and excess returns are arbitraged away.

Efficient Capital Markets and Random Walks

13.3 Tests of Market Efficiency

   Evidence From Mutual Funds:

- Studies of Mutual Funds using gross returns have shown that mutual funds do no better than to lie on the risk-return line (alpha of zero).
- Net returns (gross returns less fees) give a negative alpha.
- In an efficient market, funds with the lowest fees have the greatest alpha.

Efficient Capital Markets and Random Walks

13.3 Tests of Market Efficiency

   Evidence on Individual Investors:

- A study of 60,000 individual accounts at a discount brokerage firm showed that trading costs negatively and significantly affect the returns of market participants.
- Investors can improve returns by reducing transactions costs to the lowest level possible.

Chapter 14

Bond Valuation and Interest Rates

Bond Valuation and Interest Rates

Chapter Objectives

- Bonds - their structure and risks
- How bonds are issued in the primary market and traded in the secondary markets
- How to value a bond
- Interest rates and how interest rates affect bond valuation

---

Bond Valuation and Interest Rates

Chapter Overview

- 14.1   Bonds in General
- 14.2   Bonds and Risk
- 14.3   Types of Bonds and Trading Activity
- 14.4   Interest Rates, Default Risk, Other Factors and Bond Yields
- 14.5   Valuing a Bond

Bond Valuation and Interest Rates

14.1 Bonds in General

▪ A bond is a debt financial contract under which the issuer is obligated to make periodic interest payments and repay the principal at some pre-determined time

▪ The legal agreement between the issuer of the bonds and the investors is known as indenture

▪ The amount that is originally borrowed and the amount that is repaid when the bonds mature and the principal payment is due is known as principal value, or par amount or a maturity value

---

Bond Valuation and Interest Rates

Structure of Interest Payments on Bonds:

▪ The coupon rate or interest rate on a bond is the rate, expressed on a percentage basis, at which interest accrues or is paid by the issuer to the owner of the bond

▪ Interest rate setting structures vary and can be broadly classified into two categories

- Fixed Rate Structures

- Floating Rate Structures

▪ Interest rate setting structures affect the value of a bond

---

Bond Valuation and Interest Rates

Fixed Rate Structures:

▪ The coupon rate and payments are fixed over the life of the bond, and the investors and the issuer are certain of the payments

▪ In a Fixed Rate Par Bond, the issuer issues the bond at par value and pays fixed interest semi annually on predetermined dates and repays the full par value of the bond on maturity

Bond Valuation and Interest Rates

Fixed Rate Structures:

- In a <u>Fixed Rate Discount Bond</u>, the bond is issued at a coupon rate that creates a market value of less than par at the time of pricing, and offering an yield that is higher than the coupon rate
- In a <u>Fixed Rate Premium Bond</u>, the issuer will market a bond with a coupon and interest rate that creates a market value of more than par at the time of pricing, and an offering yield that is lower than the coupon rate

Bond Valuation and Interest Rates

Floating Rate Structures:

- In <u>floating interest rate</u> instruments, initially interest rate setting mechanisms were based upon some interest rate index or level of a risk free security
- Over the years, rate setting mechanisms have been developed that are designed to create a bond that always trades at or near par value
- Historically, the floating interest rates have been significantly lower than the rates on fixed-coupon bonds. However, the issuer retains the <u>interest rate risk</u> inherent in a bond issue

Bond Valuation and Interest Rates

Security:

- The sources of security on a bond issue can vary a great deal, and will affect the credit rating and creditworthiness of the issue
- Securities that are issued by the <u>U.S. Government</u> are usually assumed to be <u>risk-free</u>
- <u>Municipal bonds</u> may be secured in a variety of ways such as by the issuer's taxing power, revenues and credit enhancement devices

Bond Valuation and Interest Rates

Security:

- **Corporate debt** is most often an unsecured promise by the corporation to pay its debts. Sometimes the bonds will be secured by collateral or a mortgage on a particular property or piece of equipment
- **Asset-backed securities** are secured by the sponsor who structures the financing and usually purchases credit enhancement

Bond Valuation and Interest Rates

Optional Redemption:

- **Call Option:** Issuer's option to redeem bonds prior to their stated maturity, at a pre-determined price above par value
- **Call Premium:** The excess amount of the call price above the par value
- An investor that owns a **callable bond** is subject to considerable uncertainty about cash flows on its callable bonds and hence will require a higher yield on callable bonds than on comparable non-callable bonds

Bond Valuation and Interest Rates

14.2 Bonds and Risk

Four types of risk involved while investing in fixed-rate or fixed-coupon debt obligations are:

- **Default risk** - the risk that the bond will not pay interest or principal when due
- **Reinvestment risk** - the unknown rate at which cash inflows may be reinvested
- **Prepayment risk** - when an issuer calls a bond prior to its maturity
- **Interest rate risk** - the risk that a change in market interest rates will affect the value of the bond

Bond Valuation and Interest Rates

Default Risk and Bond Ratings:

- All taxable fixed-rate debt that is issued or traded in the U.S. capital markets is priced at what is called a spread to Treasuries which is the measure of default risk on an asset-backed transaction or a specific company's debt
- The interest rate, or yield, of all debt is vitally dependent on the risk-free rate associated with the comparable maturity U.S. Treasury debt
- This spread will change over time depending on economic conditions and the relative default risk associated with the specific debt security

---

Bond Valuation and Interest Rates

Spread to Treasuries

- The difference between the yield on a non-callable U.S. Treasury bond and the yield on a non-callable corporate bond with an identical maturity is called the spread to Treasuries and is a measure of the default premium associated with the corporate bond
- The spread to Treasuries is a function of the type of industry the issuer belongs, the credit rating of the corporate bond and a function of the time to maturity of the bond

---

Bonds Online Corporate Yield Curve-www.bonds-online.com/ (8/29/03)

Reuters Corporate Spreads for Banks

Spreads compiled using [Reuters Evaluators ▾] [Refresh] Download spreads

Rating	1 yr	2 yr	3 yr	5 yr	7 yr	10 yr	30 yr
Aaa/AAA	21	24	35	42	57	69	89
Aa1/AA+	30	39	40	51	67	80	100
Aa2/AA	32	45	47	55	70	82	103
Aa3/AA-	34	48	49	60	74	86	112
A1/A+	58	64	68	75	90	104	127
A2/A	61	67	70	77	92	106	131
A3/A-	65	70	73	81	95	109	132
Baa1/BBB+	78	89	97	106	138	160	186
Baa2/BBB	81	97	105	113	143	166	191
Baa3/BBB-	88	102	110	117	148	173	196
Ba1/BB+	525	535	545	555	575	595	615
Ba2/BB	535	545	555	565	585	605	625
Ba3/BB-	545	555	565	575	595	615	635
B1/B+	690	700	710	740	720	820	870
B2/B	700	710	720	750	790	830	880
B3/B-	710	720	730	760	800	840	890
Caa/CCC	1110	1120	1130	1155	1165	1175	1205

Bond Valuation and Interest Rates

Default Risk and Bond Ratings:

- Three rating agencies - Moody's Investors Services, Standard & Poor's Corporation, and Fitch Ratings Ltd. specialize in rating the default risk and credit worthiness of a bond issue and of corporate, municipal, and even sovereign government issuers
- The agencies then assign the issue with a bond rating that ranges from the equivalent of AAA, the highest grade with a very remote chance of default, down to CCC, the lowest grade and currently in default
- The ratings have significant bearing on the required yield on a bond in the marketplace

---

Bond Ratings

TABLE I Bond Ratings by Moody's and Standard and Poor's

Rating			
Moody's	Standard and Poor's	Description	Examples of Corporations with Bonds Outstanding in 2002
Aaa	AAA	Highest quality (lowest default risk)	General Electric, Pfizer Inc., Road Management Services Inc.
Aa	AA	High quality	Hewlett-Packard, Mobil Oil, Unocal Inc., Wal-Mart
A	A	Upper medium grade	Anheuser-Busch, McDonalds Inc., Motorola Inc.
Baa	BBB	Medium grade	Albertson's, Ford Motor, Marriott
Ba	BB	Lower medium grade	Rite Aid Corp., Bayer Inc., Six Flags Theme Park
B	B	Speculative	Revlon, Mary Kay Inc., U.S. Can Inc.
Caa	CCC, CC	Poor (high default risk)	U.S. Airways Inc.
Ca	C	Highly speculative	McDonnll
C	D	Lowest grade	Kmart, Carmike Cinemas, Enron

Bond Valuation and Interest Rates

Default Risk and Bond Ratings:

- Beyond the corporate credit risk rating is the risk classification specific to a particular bond issue of the company
- Senior debt is usually the most secure debt issued by a company. In the event of liquidation in bankruptcy, the most senior debt is paid first and whatever is leftover is distributed to the rest of the debt holders
- Subordinated debt is debt that follows senior debt in line for claims on cash flows and assets upon liquidation

Bond Valuation and Interest Rates

Reinvestment Risk:

- <u>Reinvestment risk</u> is the risk that arises from reinvesting the periodic interest payments on fixed-rate bonds
- An investor receiving payments over the life of a coupon-bearing bond faces the risk of reinvesting coupon payments at uncertain future interest rates than may be lower than the yield on the bond
- The yield to maturity on coupon bonds depends significantly on the reinvestment rates

---

Bond Valuation and Interest Rates

Prepayment Risk:

- <u>Prepayment risk</u> is the risk that a bond will be retired or redeemed at a time earlier than its maturity date
- The call options and redemption features in debt instruments introduce uncertainty into the expected cash flows. This uncertainty has a cost, in the way of a higher rate of interest on the bonds

---

Bond Valuation and Interest Rates

Interest Rate Risk:

- <u>Interest rate risk</u> is often the most difficult risk to assess
- The price volatility of a bond is the extent to which its price changes with fluctuations in market levels of interest rates
- Bond prices and yields move in opposite directions, other things being equal. The magnitude of price movements will differ based on specific bond characteristics

Bond Valuation and Interest Rates

Interest Rate Risk:

The <u>longer the maturity</u> of a bond, the higher the volatility of bond prices, the <u>greater the risk</u>

The table below gives the price change for a 1% increase in yield:

Maturity	Coupon	Yield	Price	% Change
10	6%	7%	$92.89	-7.11%
20	6%	7%	$89.32	-10.68%
30	6%	7%	$87.53	-12.47%

Bond Valuation and Interest Rates

Interest Rate Risk:

The <u>lower the coupon</u> on a bond, the higher the price volatility, the <u>greater the risk</u>

The table below gives the price change for a 1% increase in yield:

Coupon	Yield	Price	Yield	Price	% Change
0%	6%	$16.97	7%	$12.69	-25.23%
6%	6%	$100.00	7%	$87.53	-12.47%
12%	6%	$183.02	7%	$162.36	-11.29%

Bond Valuation and Interest Rates

Duration:

- The <u>price volatility</u> of a debt issue is measured using <u>duration</u>
- The <u>duration</u> of a bond is measured in <u>units of time</u> (for example, 7.3 years).
- In the simplest case, the duration of a zero coupon bond is equal to its current time to maturity
- The <u>higher the current coupon</u> payments, the lower the price volatility and the <u>shorter the duration</u>

Bond Valuation and Interest Rates

Duration:

Duration is also defined as a percentage change in the price of an asset, divided by a change in interest rates, and can be represented by the following equation:

$$D = \frac{-\Delta P / P}{\Delta y}$$

Where: D = Duration, P = dollar price of a bond, ΔP = change in dollar price of a bond, y = market yield, and Δy = change in market yield

- **There is an inverse relationship between interest rate movements and bond prices**

Bond Valuation and Interest Rates

Yield Curve:

- The yield curve is the relationship between the yields and the maturities on Treasury securities.
- The yield curve usually is positively sloped which means that investors require higher returns for longer maturity Treasury securities. This is because the prices of longer maturity bonds are more volatile and therefore are viewed as being riskier than shorter maturity securities

---

Typical Yield Curves

FOLLOWING THE FINANCIAL NEWS
Yield Curves

The Wall Street Journal publishes a daily plot of the yield curves for Treasury securities, an example of which is presented here. It is typically found next to the "Credit Markets" column.

The numbers on the vertical axis indicate the interest rate for the Treasury security with the maturity given by the numbers on the horizontal axis. For example, the yield curve marked "Monday" indicates that the interest rate on the three-month Treasury bill was 1.7%, while the two-year bill had an interest rate of 3.1% and the ten-year bond had an interest rate of 5.1%. As you can see, the yield curves in the plot has a steep upward slope.

Treasury Yield Curve
Yields as of 2:00 p.m. EST on Monday.
The bond market closed on New Year's day.

Dynamic yield curve that can show the curve at any time in history
http://stockcharts.com/charts/YieldCurve.html

191

Bond Valuation and Interest Rates

14.3 Types of Bonds and Trading Activity

Treasury Securities and the Treasury Market:

- The market for U.S. Treasury securities is the largest and most liquid of any financial markets
- Treasury notes have maturities of one-to-seven years, and bonds have maturities of over seven years
- These securities pay interest on a semi-annual basis over the life the issue, and then the investor gets the principle back at maturity
- Treasury securities' prices fluctuate daily in response to changes in interest rates and the economy

---

Bloomberg Treasury Yield Curve (8/29/03)

Notes/Bonds

	COUPON	MATURITY DATE	CURRENT PRICE/YIELD	PRICE/YIELD CHANGE	TI
2-Year	2.000	08/31/2005	100-02/1.96	-0-02/0.032	2
3-Year	2.375	08/15/2006	99-22/2.49	-0-03/0.033	2
5-Year	3.250	08/15/2008	99-02/3.45	-0-07/0.052	2
10-Year	4.250	08/15/2013	98-11/4.46	-0-11/0.044	2
30-Year	5.375	02/15/2031	102-07/5.22	-0-07/0.015	2

Bond Valuation and Interest Rates

Municipal Bonds and the Municipal Market:

- <u>Municipal bonds</u> are debt instruments issued by states, cities, municipal authorities and other entities
- Municipal bond interest income is <u>exempt from federal and certain state and local income taxation</u>
- Investor can compare Municipal Bonds interest income with after-tax income of other fixed-income securities, taking into account the investor's marginal tax bracket
- The municipal bond market is a huge, diverse, and extremely complicated marketplace

Bond Valuation and Interest Rates

Municipal Bonds Example:

An investor in the 30% tax bracket purchases a municipal bond that pays a tax-exempt interest rate of 6%. Calculate the taxable equivalent municipal bond yield

$$\underline{\text{Taxable Equivalent Bond Yield}} = \frac{r}{1-t} = \frac{6.00}{(1-0.3)} = 8.6\%$$

Bond Valuation and Interest Rates

Taxable Bonds and the Taxable Bond Market:

- Corporations issue bonds to finance their long-term capital needs and to take advantage of tax deduction associated with the interest payments on debt
- Bonds are issued in the primary market at a yield based on the spread to Treasuries that is required for an issue with the appropriate risk
- Corporations also issue bonds known as <u>convertible bonds</u> that usually pays a fixed-rate of interest, and after a certain period of time, can be converted into a fixed number of shares of the issuing corporation

---

Bond Valuation and Interest Rates

Taxable Bonds and the Taxable Bond Market:

- <u>Mortgage-backed bonds</u> and the <u>asset-backed bonds</u>, secured by car loans, credit card receivables, and other structured bond issues are usually created by financial institutions that originate the loans that are then pooled and marketed to institutional investors
- These bonds are sold to investors in the primary market through an investment banking syndicate and are traded in the secondary over-the counter market

Bond Valuation and Interest Rates

14.4 Interest Rates, Default Risk, Other Factors and   Bond Yields

The yield or return that an investor should expect to receive on a financial asset such as a bond is a function of a number of factors, the most important of which are:
- The time value of money
- The default risk associated with a particular security
- The liquidity premium and other bond specific factors peculiar to the financial asset, such as call provisions

---

Bond Valuation and Interest Rates

The Term Structure of Interest Rates:

- The yield curve, also known as the term structure of interest rates, describes the relationship between the yield on a security and its maturity
- The shape of the yield curve, depending on the rate of inflation or deflation, the economy and monetary policies, can be upward sloping - which is the most common, downward sloping - when a significant slowdown in inflation is anticipated, flat, or humped

---

Bond Valuation and Interest Rates

The Term Structure of Interest Rates:

- Several hypotheses attempt to explain the term structure of interest rates and the information that it conveys to the market
- The three most common explanations are:
  - Pure expectations hypothesis
  - The liquidity preference hypothesis
  - The market segmentation hypothesis

Bond Valuation and Interest Rates

Pure Expectations Hypothesis:

- Under <u>Pure expectations hypothesis</u> the yield curve can be analyzed as a series of expected future short-term interest rates that will adjust in a way such that investors will receive equivalent holding period returns
- Thus the expected average annual return on a long-term bond is the compound average of the expected short-term interest rates
- Thus an upward-sloping yield curve means that investors expect higher future short-term interest rates and a downward-sloping yield curve implies expectations of lower future short-term rates

Bond Valuation and Interest Rates

The Liquidity Preference Hypothesis :

- According to the <u>liquidity preference theory</u> most investors prefer to hold short-term maturity securities and hence in order to induce investors to hold bonds with longer maturities, the issuer must pay a higher interest rate as a liquidity premium
- Thus under this theory, long-term rates are composed of <u>expected short-term rates plus a liquidity premium which increases with time to maturity</u>
- This theory implies an upward-sloping yield curve even when investors expect that short-term rates will remain constant

Relationship Between the Liquidity Premium and Pure Expectations Theory

Bond Valuation and Interest Rates

The Market Segmentation Hypothesis :

- The <u>market segmentation hypothesis</u> or the preferred habitat hypothesis, recognizes that the market is composed of diverse investors who have different preferred habitats i.e. short term and long term investments for the investment requirements
- In order to induce investors to move away from their preferred position on the yield curve, an issuer must pay a premium. Thus any maturities that do not have a balance of supply and demand will sell at a premium or discount to their expected yields and the shape of the yield curve is dependent upon demand and supply

---

Bond Valuation and Interest Rates

Yield Curve as a Predictor of Short-Term Rates:

- Based on empirical evidence, the yield curve has been a particularly poor predictor of future short-term interest rates
- However the rates implied by the pure expectations model of the yield curve is important because trading activity can effectively lock in the forward and zero-coupon rates that are implied in the yield curve, the yield discount rates can be used to value cash flows associated with bonds and valuation of derivatives

---

Bond Valuation and Interest Rates

The Yield Curve, Inflation and Deflation:

- <u>Nominal interest rate</u> is the actual rate of return or yield associated with an investment (not adjusting for the effect of inflation or deflation)
- The <u>real rate of interest</u> is defined as the difference between the nominal rate of interest and the rate of inflation

  Example: If inflation is 2% and nominal interest rate of 10 year Treasury bond is 6%, then:

  real rate of interest = 6% - 2% = 4%

Bond Valuation and Interest Rates

Call Features and Other Factors:

- The yield level on a bond is influenced by its liquidity, call features and other factors
- With greater liquidity the bonds are more marketable and there is less of a liquidity yield premium associated with the bond
- Investors analyzing a corporate, municipal, or asset-backed bond assign a premium in the way of a higher interest rate to reflect any optional and extraordinary call provisions in the issue

---

Bond Valuation and Interest Rates

Calculating Bond Yield:

- A bond is valued by discounting bond's cash flows at the yield level that is required by securities of comparable maturity, risk, liquidity and call features. Hence, the computation of a required yield level is a function of all of these factors
- The yield on a risky security can be represented by the yield on a comparable maturity risk-free security, plus a measure of the spread to Treasuries for default risk, plus a bond specific spread i.e.
- *Bond Yield = R_f + Spread to Treas. + Bond Specific Spread*

Bond Valuation and Interest Rates

14.5 Valuing a Bond:

- <u>Two important facts</u> associated with valuation and bond prices in the marketplace are:
- <u>Bond prices and changes in interest rates move in opposite directions</u>
- <u>Investors and traders value and bonds based on a price to worst call feature scenario</u>; i.e. issuer of the bond will act in its own best interest in calling or managing the bond's call features and will exercise the call at the first available opportunity that is economically advantageous to the issuer

Bond Valuation and Interest Rates

Valuing a Bond – Example:

- Let us value the bond of XYZ Inc. which has a face value of $1000, maturity of 10 years and pays interest semi-annually at a coupon rate of 8%
- We calculate the cash flows from the bond

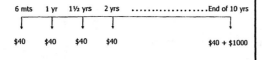

| 6 mts | 1 yr | 1½ yrs | 2 yrs | .... End of 10 yrs |
| $40 | $40 | $40 | $40 | $40 + $1000 |

Bond Valuation and Interest Rates

Using a Financial Calculator to Value a Bond:

- Take an example of a 10 year bond than pays interest semi annually at 10% and interest rates for a 10-year bond of similar risk is 9%, calculate the value of the bond
- We input values in the financial calculator:

  n = 20 (since payments are received semi annually)

  pmt = $50

  i = 4.5% (semi-annual interest rate)

  fv = $1000

  Then solve for PV which is equal to $1065.04

Bond Valuation and Interest Rates

Valuing a Bond – Discount Bond Example:

- If the interest rates for an 8% coupon, 10-year bond of comparable risk were at 10%, we discount the $40 pmt at 10% (5% semi);

  n=20, i=5%, pmt=40, fv=1000, solve for pv=$875.38

- The market price of this bond is below or at a discount to its face value and is known as a discount bond
- A discount bond has a coupon that is lower than its yield

Bond Valuation and Interest Rates

Valuing a Bond – Par Bond Example:

- The yield for a 10-year bond is 8% and the coupon rate is 8%. We discount the cash flows at 8%;
- N=20, i=4%, pmt= 40, fv=1000, solve for pv=$1000 which is the face value of the bond

- A bond in which its coupon rate is <u>equal</u> to its yield has a price equal to its face value and is known as a <u>Par Bond</u>

Bond Valuation and Interest Rates

Valuing a Bond – Non-Callable Premium Bond Example:

- The interest rates for a 10-year, 8% coupon bond with a face value of $1000 drops to 7%. What's its value?
  n=20, i=3. 5%, pmt=40, fv=1000, pv=<u>$1071.06</u>

- A bond in which its coupon rate is <u>lower</u> than the yield required by the market has a market price <u>higher</u> than its face value and is known as a <u>Premium Bond</u>

Bond Valuation and Interest Rates

Valuing a Callable Premium Bond to Call Date:

- Let assume that the bond is callable after 5 years at 101% of par value
- Since the bond is callable by the issuer we price it on the *price to worst* scenario, which assumes the issuer will call the bond when it makes economic sense
- Hence if the issuer calls the bond after 5 years at 101% of par value, the value of the bond is:
- n=10, pmt=$50, i=4.5% & fv=1010 pv=<u>$1046.00</u>
- The value of a callable bond is the lower of the price to call-<u>$1046</u> or the price to maturity $1065.06.

Chapter 15

How to Value a Stock

How to Value a Stock

Chapter Objectives

- How to value a stock
- Discuss various approaches to stock valuation
- Discuss how to use the stock valuation program, ValuePro, and how to use the website Valuepro.net to value stocks

---

How to Value a Stock

Chapter Overview

- 15.1   Introduction to Stock Valuation
- 15.2   Return to Stockholders
- 15.3   Stock Valuation Approaches: Fundamental, Technical and MPT
- 15.4   The Discounted Free Cash Flow to the Firm Valuation Approach
- 15.5   Valuepro.net Online Stock Valuation Web Site

How to Value a Stock

15.1 Introduction to Stock Valuation

- Common stock represents a proportionate ownership interest in a corporation
- The <u>value</u> of a stock depends on the firm's future <u>profits</u> or cash flows and the <u>rate of return</u> or required yield is expected from the investment
- <u>Higher profits increase</u> a stock's <u>market value</u> and lower profits decrease its value—a <u>direct relationship</u>
- <u>Higher interest rates decrease market value</u> and lower yields and interest rates increase value—an <u>inverse relationship</u>.

How to Value a Stock

15.1 Introduction to Stock Valuation

- A stock is valued in the same manner as other financial asset—discount its expected cash flows at a risk-adjusted discount rate.
- The range of future cash flows for a stock can be enormous. Cash flows can be higher or lower than expected. We make simplifying assumptions regarding the expected cash flows.
- A corporation is a legal entity that has an infinite life and the valuation procedure must address the issue of valuing cash flows to infinity.

How to Value a Stock

15.1 Introduction to Stock Valuation

- An asset that has a stream of even cash flows that continue to infinity is known as a <u>perpetuity</u>
- The value of a perpetuity is calculated by dividing the level annual cash flow associated with the perpetuity by the discounting rate:

Value of a Perpetuity = $\dfrac{\text{Annual Cash Flow}}{\text{Discounting Rate}}$

How to Value a Stock

15.2   Return to Stockholders

- Return to stockholders includes any dividend payments plus the increase (or minus the decrease) in stock price that investors experience during an investment holding period

% Return to Stockholders = (Dividends + Change in Stock Price)
                                        Beginning Stock Price

- For example, if a stock's price started the year at $100, the stock paid $1 in dividends during the year, and it ended the year at $109, its percentage annual return to stockholders equals: ($1 + $9)/ $100 = 10%.

How to Value a Stock

Stock Value and Dividend Policy:

- The dividend policy of the firm should not affect the current value of a stock.
- However, the expected future value of a stock is greatly affected by dividend policy.
- When a company does not pay dividends and reinvests its earnings in projects, the investors receive no current dividend but instead receive an increase in stock price.

XYZ Dividend Company—Stock price stays constant—Investors receive 10% Dividend Return

Table 15-1

XYZ Dividend Company-Stock Price Change

100% Dividend Payment

Year	Market Equity	Earnings	Required Return	Dividend	Net Invest	Stock Price
1	$1 billion	$100 million	10%	$100 million	0	$10
2	$1 billion	$100 million	10%	$100 million	0	$10
3	$1 billion	$100 million	10%	$100 million	0	$10

UVW Growth Company—Stock price increases 10% per year—Investors receive No Dividends

Table 15-2						
UVW Growth Company-Stock Price						
0% Dividend Payment						
	Market		Required		Net	Stock
Year	Equity	Earnings	Return	Dividend	Invest	Price
1	$1 billion	$100 million	10%	0	$100 million	10.00
2	$1.1 billion	$110 million	10%	0	$110 million	11.00
3	$1.21 billion	$121 million	10%	0	$121 million	12.10

How to Value a Stock

15.3 Stock Valuation Approaches

▪Professional stock market participants practice a number of investment approaches and techniques which is classified as fitting into one of three camps: Fundamental Analysis, Technical Analysis, and Modern Portfolio Theory (MPT)

▪ The three philosophies have different beliefs about the relationship between the stock prices that we observe in the markets and underlying intrinsic stock values

---

How to Value a Stock

Exhibit 15-1
Valuation Strategies
How to Value a Share?

	Technical Analysis	Fundamental Analysis	Portfolio Theory
What Drives Stock Prices?	Psychology Technical Cosmic	Earnings Dividends	Risk & Return
How to Value A Share?	Trends Waves Factors	Forecast Dividends & Earnings	Risk & Return
Relationship Between Value and Prices?	P ≠ V	P will Eventually Equal Value	P = V

How to Value a Stock

Technical Analysis

- Technical analysts believe that stock prices are influenced more by investor psychology and emotions of the crowd than by changes in the fundamentals of the company.

- Technical analysts chart historic stock price movements, volume of trading activity, and the price/volume aspects of related equity and debt markets to predict or anticipate the stock buying behavior of other market participants.

- Technical analysts generally have a shorter-term stock holding orientation and more frequent trading activity.

Sample TA Chart for Microsoft vs. NASDAQ

How to Value a Stock

Fundamental Analysis

- According to Fundamental Analysis approach, the company's current and future operating and financial performance determine the value of the company's stock

- The assumption underlying this approach is that a company's stock has a true or intrinsic value to which its price is anchored. When there is an price divergence, the price over time will gravitate to its intrinsic value.

- To assess a company's prospects, fundamental analysts evaluate overall economic, industry and company data to estimate a stock's value

How to Value a Stock

Fundamental Analysis – Target Stock Price

- Examples of fundamental analysis approach include DCF valuation, target stock price and relative valuation.
- Target Stock Price technique forecasts earnings per share (EPS) of a firm and multiplies EPS by the projected P/E ratio to arrive at a target stock price.
- Example: Suppose the projected EPS of XYZ Inc. is $2.50 and the market P/E ratio is 10. The target stock price of XYZ Inc. is $25. If the current market price of the stock is $20, a financial analyst would recommend buying the stock.

How to Value a Stock

Fundamental Analysis – Relative Valuation

- Relative value analysis employ measures of value such as P/E ratios, price/book values (P/BV), price/sales (P/S), or the price/earnings/growth (PEG) ratios for a company and compares them with those of similar stocks and industry peers
- Example: "McDonalds current P/E of 15.8 is below the P/Es of other fast food restaurant chains. Given that the company's growth in earnings and sales is in line with industry peers, and its risk profile is below that of its competitors, we conclude that McDonalds is undervalued"

How to Value a Stock

Fundamental Analysis – DCF Valuation

- In the DCF approach a stock's value is the sum of the expected cash flows of the company, discounted at an appropriate interest rate.
- The most basic DCF approach is the dividend discount model (DDM), under which an analyst estimates future dividend growth and the required rate of return on the stock and discounts those expected dividends to arrive at a stock's value.
- Other DCF approaches are the free cash flow to equity (FCFE) model and free cash flow to the firm (FCFF) model.

How to Value a Stock

Modern Portfolio Theory

- Efficient capital markets is a cornerstone of MPT and is the belief that stock prices always reflect intrinsic value, and that any type of fundamental or technical analysis is already embedded in the stock price.
- As such, MPT devotees tell investors not to bother to search for undervalued stocks but instead to pick a risk level that they can live with and diversify holdings among a portfolio of stocks.
- However empirical evidence shows that there is value to careful stock selection.

My Valuation Philosophy

There is value to careful stock selection (FA).

Timing of purchase and sale of stock is important (TA).

Diversification is good (MPT).

Value each stock holding individually and buy shares that are undervalued by (15)% and sell shares that are overvalued by (15)%

How to Value a Stock

Free Cash Flow to the Firm Valuation Approach

The discounted free cash flow to the firm valuation approach is a four-step process to value the stock of a company

Step 1: Forecast the company's Expected Cash Flow

Step 2: Estimate its Weighted Average Cost of Capital

Step 3: Calculate the Enterprise Value of the Company

Step 4: Calculate Intrinsic Stock Value

How to Value a Stock

Excess Return Period and Competitive Advantage

- The Excess Return Period is the period during which a company is able to earn returns on new investments that are greater than its cost of capital because of a competitive advantage enjoyed by the firm.

- Success attracts competitors and over time a company loses its competitive advantage and the return from its new investments just equals its WACC (i.e. investors are just compensated for the risk that they are taking in owning the company's stock and no additional value is created from new business investments).

How to Value a Stock

Excess Return Period and Competitive Advantage

Depending upon the excess return period companies can be grouped into 4 categories:

<u>Boring companies</u> - operate in a highly competitive, low-margin industry - a 1 year excess return period

<u>Decent companies</u> - decent reputation, don't control pricing or growth in their industry - a 5 year excess return period

<u>Good companies</u> - good brand names, large economies of scale - a 7 year excess return period

<u>Great companies</u> - great growth potential, tremendous marketing power, brand names - a 10 year excess return period

---

How to Value a Stock

Residual Value

- Once a company loses its competitive advantage the stock price of the company still grows in value, but its growth does not exceed its risk-adjusted market expectation of the investors.

- At that point in time, the after-tax earnings of the company can be treated and valued as what is known as a cash flow perpetuity—equal to the company's net operating profit after tax divided by its WACC. This discounted value is called the company's <u>residual value</u>.

- Residual value is very important—it generally represents 60% to 90% of the company's stock value.

How to Value a Stock

15.6   Valuepro.net Online Stock Valuation Web Site

- The Web site www.valuepro.net is devoted to the DCF method of stock valuation and has links that explain the approach in detail.
- Type a stock symbol into the slot on the home Web page, click on the Get Baseline Valuation button, and the online valuation program accesses data sources for information relating to the company that you are valuing and calculates   twenty variables, puts them into a valuation algorithm and   calculates the intrinsic stock value of the company using a   simple discounted cash flow model.

How to Value a Stock

15.6   Valuepro.net Online Stock Valuation Web Site

ValuePro

Announcing ValuePro 2002 Software!!

▷ Home
▷ Learn the ValuePro Approach
▷ Streetsmart Guide to Valuing a Stock
▷ Buy Streetsmart Guide
▷ Buy ValuePro 2002 Software
▷ Guide to the ValuePro 2002 Software
▷ Buy Running With the Bulls
▷ Frequently Asked Questions
▷ Message Board
▷ Contact Us
▷ Terms of Service
▷ About the Online Valuation

Thank you for your patience during our recent site downtime. We have improved not only the efficiency of our valuation scripts, but also, our newly-hosted and online payment processing, which is now up and running.

ValuePro 2002 is our new easy-to-use stock valuation program that interacts with our online valuation service. Now you can download data from our web site to your computer and use ValuePro 2002 to analyze your investments. The price is only $44.50. Please see our Guide to the ValuePro 2002 Software for an in-depth description.

Try our online stock valuation service. Enter the stock symbol, click on the Get Baseline Valuation button, and see do the rest. The inputs used to value the stock are updated periodically. You can change any input and revaluate a stock value. Learn more about using the online valuation by clicking here.

Enter Stock Symbol [   ]   Get Baseline Valuation

We are developing a stock value/stock price screening program which will rank stocks based upon a value-to-price ratio and a portfolio valuation program.

Value Screening   Portfolio Valuation

ValuePro.net was founded by three financial engineers/finance professors to develop and distribute inexpensive, easy to use and understand valuation tools.

1443712 hits since June 1, 2000

How to Value a Stock

15.6   Valuepro.net Online Stock Valuation Web Site

- You can go to any or all of the input cells, put your own estimates into the cells, hit the Recalculate button, and the online valuation program calculates the new intrinsic stock value based on the inputs that you have provided
- If you want to see the detailed pro forma statement associated with the valuation, click on the Cash Flows button and a cash flow schedule based on the underlying inputs appears

Valuation of Microsoft

Use valuepro.net online valuation service to get general input page and cash flow page.

Look at price sensitivity to Growth Rate, NOPMs, and Interest Rates.

Chapter 16

Management of Risk - Diversifying, Hedging, Insuring and Derivative Securities

---

Management of Risk: Diversifying, Hedging, Insuring and Derivative Securities

Chapter objectives

- The risk of financial assets and how that risk can be managed;

- The process of diversification;

- Hedging and how it can be done effectively;

- Derivative securities and how they may be used to reduce risk.

Management of Risk: Diversifying, Hedging, Insuring and Derivative Securities

Chapter overview

- 16.1 The management of risk

- 16.2 Diversification– the costless way to reduce risk

- 16.3 Hedging– sacrifice gain to protect against loss

- 16.4 Insurance– pay a premium to protect against loss

- 16.5 Derivative securities

Management of Risk: Diversifying, Hedging, Insuring and Derivative Securities

16.1 The management of risk

- Risk is usually measured by the volatility of the rate of return, such as standard deviation
- Trade off between risk and return:
  The higher the return, the higher the risk

Asset Class	Ibbotson & Sinquefield Study		
	Compound Annual Return	Simple Average Annual Return	Std. Dev. of Return
U.S. Treasury Bills	3.80%	3.90%	3.20%
U.S. Treasury Bonds	5.30%	5.70%	9.40%
Corporate Bonds	5.60%	6.10%	8.60%
Large Company Stocks	10.70%	12.70%	20.20%
Small Company Stocks	12.50%	17.30%	33.20%

Management of Risk: Diversifying, Hedging, Insuring and Derivative Securities

16.1 The management of risk

- Investors are usually risk averse
- Ways to reduce risk associated with financial assets
  - Diversification
    - Spread the risk by investing in a number of risky assets
  - Hedging
    - By using techniques to lock-in a price or return
  - Insurance
    - Pay a premium to purchase a contract to protect
  - Sell the assets

Management of Risk: Diversifying, Hedging, Insuring and Derivative Securities

16.2 Diversification– the costless way to reduce risk

- As long as the returns of assets are not perfectly correlated, diversification acts to reduce risk
- Correlation
  - Measures the degree to which the movement of variables are related, and can range between -1.0 to 1.0
  - Correlation of 1.0 means when one stock up 10%, the other stock also up 10%
  - Correlation of -1.0 means when one stock up 10%, the other stock down 10%
  - Assets that are highly correlated offer less risk reduction

Management of Risk: Diversifying, Hedging, Insuring and Derivative Securities

16.2 Diversification– the costless way to reduce risk

- Stockholders face two types of risk: systematic risk and unsystematic risk

  Total Risk = Systematic Risk + Unsystematic Risk

- Systematic risk
  - Represents the risk of the stock market
  - It is caused by economy, taxes, and other market factors
  - It can not be diversified away
- Unsystematic risk
  - Is specific to a company
  - Diversification reduces the unsystematic risk

Management of Risk: Diversifying, Hedging, Insuring and Derivative Securities

16.2 Diversification– the costless way to reduce risk

- Diversification is easy to obtain in a portfolio
- Achieving the highest return for certain level of risk is known as investing on the efficient frontier
- Studies show that 20—25 stocks are sufficient to reduce risk

Number of Stocks in Portfolio	Average Standard Deviation of Annual Portfolio Returns	Ratio of Portfolio Standard Deviation of a Single Stock
1	49.24%	100%
10	23.93%	49%
50	20.20%	41%
100	19.69%	40%
300	19.34%	39%
500	19.27%	39%
1000	19.21%	39%

Management of Risk: Diversifying, Hedging, Insuring and Derivative Securities

16.3 Hedging – sacrifice gain to protect against loss

- There are three types of hedging instruments
  - Future contracts
    - A forward contract with standardized terms that trades on an organized exchange
  - Forward contracts
    - A written agreement between two parties that is not traded on an organized exchange
  - Swaps
    - An agreement between two or more parties to exchange sets of cash flows over a period of time
    - Interest swap and currency swap

Management of Risk: Diversifying, Hedging,
Insuring and Derivative Securities

16.3 Hedging – sacrifice gain to protect against loss

- Some terms relating to hedging
  - Hedgers and speculators
  - Long position and short position
  - Value and size of a contract
  - Spot price and forward price
- When an investor hedges, he fixes the sales price for the asset and gives up any upside gain for offloading the risk of loss.

Management of Risk: Diversifying, Hedging,
Insuring and Derivative Securities

16.4 Insurance– pay a premium to protect against loss

- Insurance contracts
  - Cap-Limitation of the amount of money paid under a claim
  - Deductibles
- Option
  - Financial assets that have characteristics similar to insurance contracts
  - Represents the right to sell or purchase an asset at a fixed price at a fixed time in the future

---

Management of Risk: Diversifying, Hedging,
Insuring and Derivative Securities

16.4 Insurance– pay a premium to protect against loss

Option
- Strike price
  - Also known as exercise price, predetermined
- Expiration date
  - After which the option can no longer be exercised
- Call option
  - Call option contracts enable the owner to buy an asset
- Put option
  - Put option contracts enables the owner to sell an asset

Management of Risk: Diversifying, Hedging, Insuring and Derivative Securities

16.4 Insurance– pay a premium to protect against loss

Option

S = current market price of security underlying the option
Xc = exercise price or strike price on the call option
Xp = exercise price or strike price on the put option

- The call option is in the money if S >Xc
- The put option is in the money if S < *Xp*
- An option has positive value to its owner before expiration
- The price or value of a call or put option has two components:
  - Intrinsic value and Time value

Management of Risk: Diversifying, Hedging, Insuring and Derivative Securities

16.4 Insurance– pay a premium to protect against loss

Value of Option

- Intrinsic value
  The amount the option is in the money and is the difference between the current price and the strike price of the option.

- Time value
  Reflects expectations of an option's profitability associated with exercising it at some future point in time

---

Management of Risk: Diversifying, Hedging, Insuring and Derivative Securities

16.4 Insurance– pay a premium to protect against loss

Value of Option

Example

If McDonald's stock is trading at $20 per share and the strike price of an option that expires in six months is $18, and the option is trading at a price of $3.80, the intrinsic value of the option is:

Intrinsic Value = S – Xc = $20 - $18 = $2

Time Value of Option = $3.80 - $2 = $1.80

Management of Risk: Diversifying, Hedging, Insuring and Derivative Securities

16.5 Derivative securities

Derivative securities

- Financial instruments
- Value derives from or is based on
  - The value of a simple security or
  - The level of an interest rate or
  - Interest rate index or
  - Stock market index
- Delivery occurs sometimes many years into the future, and buyer or seller can offset transactions

---

Management of Risk: Diversifying, Hedging, Insuring and Derivative Securities

16.5 Derivative securities

Derivative securities

- Many securities have features embedded in them that make them derivative securities, such as callable bonds, and convertible bonds

Value Call Option = Value Callable Bond – Value Non-Callable Bond

- Derivative securities often are more sensitive to price or yield changes, and sometimes are more leveraged
  - Attractive to hedgers
  - Can backfire for speculators

Management of Risk: Diversifying, Hedging, Insuring and Derivative Securities

16.5 Derivative securities

Derivative securities

Example

Let's assume that the 30-year bond that is callable in 10 years issued by ABC Company is trading at 100% and has an 8% coupon. Let's also assume that the yield for a non-callable 30-year bond of a company with default risk similar to ABC Company is 7%.

What's the value of the call option?

Management of Risk: Diversifying, Hedging, Insuring and Derivative Securities

16.5 Derivative securities

Derivative securities

Answer to the example

Step 1 Non-callable bond present value
   PV = $1124.72
   (Using calculator n=60, PMT=40, i=3.5 FV=1000)

Step 2 The value of callable bond $1000

Step 3 Value of the call option is
   1000- 1124.72 = -$124.72

Management of Risk: Diversifying, Hedging, Insuring and Derivative Securities

16.5 Derivative securities

Types of derivative securities

- Equity and Debt Components:
  - Embedded with the characteristics of a simple stock or bond.
  - The bond component can be fixed-rate, zero-coupon, or amortizing.

- Option or price insurance components:
  - Interest rate floors and caps, call and put options.
  - Zero or positive values are associated with these components for the *owner* of the option.
  - Zero or negative values are associated with these components for the *writer* of the option.

Management of Risk: Diversifying, Hedging, Insuring and Derivative Securities

16.5 Derivative securities

Types of derivative securities

- Hedging or price-fixing components:
  - Forward, futures contracts, interest rate and currency swap
  - The value of these components may be positive or negative, depending on movements and shifts in yields, currency levels, or spot prices.
  - The relative value at the time of issuance of the derivative security is zero.
  - Generally have little upfront cost and are the most efficient type of hedging contract.